A Storied Kingdom

Sports, culture, history, and
human-interest
stories from County Kerry

ORLA
KELLY
PUBLISHING

Tadhg Evans

Published in Ireland by Orla Kelly Publishing.

CONTENTS

About this book vii

Foreword: By Kevin Hughes, Editor of

       The Kerryman xiii

Part One: Sport.. 1

'I would do anything for that boy.' 3

A life lived in the fast lane. 7

Half-ton of gold for Glenbeigh star 14

There's much more to Pobalscoil Chorca

Dhuibhne than *just* two Hogan Cup titles. 17

Bats, balls, sun, and sandwiches.....................22

Killarney's hurling showpiece.........................29

'Give everything a chance.' 35

'This isn't a threat… this is about survival.'....43

Ready and set to face the best. 51

When Lios Póil had West Kerry in the

palm of its hand 56

Lee aiming to hit new heights at Paralympics 68

Part Two: Culture and History...................................77

Caid, craic, and the odd pint at Comórtas
Peile na Gaeltachta. 79

Oh, for the love of caid!..83

'Back then, a camera was
a mighty novelty.' 88

A centenarian's story...93

Preserving a haunting past...98

Refreshed Wexford hurler sets eyes on magical
Blasket return. 103

Ó Cinnéide takes to the field on behalf of his
treasured language. 108

The book that almost never was................................113

Living the Blasket life 117

Part Three: Fighting the Odds................................. 123

No stopping Christy's comeback. 125

'I spoke out - and that saved my life.' 130

Jack and Jill helped Hannah climb that hill. 135

Helping little Alexis reach her potential....................141

Breaking electoral barriers 146

Still smiling, still inspiring..152

Céad Míle Fáilte?..156

Flying the rainbow flag in the Kingdom 162

Reaching out to survivors of sexual violence 167

A chance encounter with absolute evil........................172

'This message is for everybody. We can't have
another Holocaust' 179

First anniversary of lock-down: how COVID
defined Kerry's news year..184

Part Four: Human Achievement................................ 193

From California to Florida on a bike 195

Why do it at all?...199

No pain, no gain, no lifelong memories.......................204

Swimming where no one dares 209

Part Five: Hard to Define 215

'Where a goat is King, and the people act the goat.' 217

Recapturing fond memories to a Heavenly
Kingdom backdrop 220

From Dublin to Kells to Chelsea 224

Broadway lights in sight for the kingdom's
Fred Astaire 229

Still competing, still winning, still enjoying. 234

A 'local' is nothing without the locals. 239

Just Kerry doing Kerry things 244

Not so sisterly. 247

Mike takes one last stop 253

Lost in the Outback: what became of
Paddy Moriarty? 257

The boy who played his
way to heaven 268

About the author 272

About this book

I'M NOT sure if there's a better-known regional title in Ireland than *The Kerryman*.

My time with this newspaper and its sister, *The Corkman*, began in May 2016, and every day since has been somewhere between slightly and wildly different from the one before. I've spent some days in our Denny Street office on a high; on other days, I haven't felt up to the pressure that comes with working in media.

But there's been one constant feeling throughout the past five years, and that's pride.

The Kerryman is one of the great names in Irish journalism, and to be a small part of its glittering 116-year history is humbling. I know that'll come across as the kind of clichéd sentence people fall back on without thinking deeply enough about something, but that's genuinely how I feel about being a part of this. Some people tell me it's just a job – but it isn't. Not to me.

I still love seeing my name in print, regardless of the weight of the story beneath it. Whether it's a cheque presentation or a two-page interview with someone I idolised growing up, it's nice to be the person doing the write-up. Every story means something to someone.

I learned that very quickly. Within my first week, a man rang me to complain about a story I'd written, and with no experience behind me, I assumed I must have been in the wrong. I remember guiltily bringing this man's gripe to my editor, Kevin Hughes, and over two or three minutes, he analysed this fella's argument and compared it against the 'offending' piece.

"I wouldn't worry about it," he said at the end. I can't remember what the piece was about, but I remember the relief I felt at knowing I'd done nothing wrong. The article was solid.

A short time later, Annascaul resident Nancy Falvey rang Kevin. I'd profiled her daughter, Hannah – and how Rett's Syndrome was affecting her young life – just days previously, and while I don't know what Nancy said on the phone to Kevin, I know it must have been glowing because Kevin himself was glowing afterwards.

I was on work experience at that time, and I sometimes wonder if Nancy's phone call convinced Kevin that I was worth taking on as a more permanent member of staff.

Since then, I've developed a particular liking for feature pieces, interviews, profiles, that kind of thing. I don't know if I'm any good at that type of writing, but when I do have a go at it, people seem to respond favourably – and that's why I've compiled the better ones, as I see them. In this book, they've been divided into four sections: Sport; Culture and History; Fighting the Odds; and Human Achievement.

A fifth section – 'Hard to define' – is also included and consists of stories that don't fall into any of the four aforementioned categories; they are, well, 'hard to define'.

Some of the pieces here have been changed from when they were printed – it's hard to hit the sweet spot first time around – though only my own writing and structuring were subject to change. Some articles have even been altered quite a bit because, well, reading back, I overdid them when I first had a go a few years back.

But the people I spoke to gave me stories that were too good not to include here and, if anything, the quotes they gave me back then won't be drowned out by my overwriting this time.

If my gratitude towards Kevin hasn't come across already, then I'll emphasise it again: I thank him. But he's not the only one I owe a good word to.

I thank, in no particular order, everyone I work with. On the editorial side, these are Paul Brennan, Simon Brouder, Fergus Dennehy, Stephen Fernane, Sinead Kelleher, Dónal Nolan, and Damian Stack. I must also mention those who've taken the photographs that have appeared alongside my stories: Michelle Cooper Galvin, Valerie O'Sullivan, Christy Riordan, and Domnick Walsh.

On the other side of the house, advertising: Geraldine Brosnan, Louise Boyle, Danny Cooper, Sandra Daw, Celine Lonergan, and former staff member Teresa O'Shea.

Tadhg Evans

I wish to thank my General Manager – Siobhán Murphy – and former Managing Director, John Feerick. I suppose he took a bit of a punt on me five years ago, at a time when I hadn't much of a CV backing me up.

I want to thank our Production Manager, Tommy King, who still seems to think I'm the go-to man on all things tennis-related. I've never given any indication that I've a passion for tennis.

He used to call me Dave.

Declan Malone does the vast majority of his work from Dingle as opposed to the Tralee office nowadays, but he has been good to me throughout my short career. It's probably because I'm from west Kerry, not because I'm any good – but whatever the case, I thank him.

I thank his brother, Brendan, and everyone at *The Corkman* office in Mallow: Bill Browne, Billy Mangan, Concubhar Ó Liatháin, and former staff member Noelle Foley.

I thank my friends from Lios Póil, also – mainly the ones who were in my year, but also a few others in the years above and below mine. There are too many to mention individually, but I'll make an exception for Dara Moriarty; look it, I suppose we all have a 'best' friend.

I thank Orla Kelly Publishing and Emma Prendiville of Blank Slate Ireland. Without Orla, the product you're holding wouldn't exist, and without Emma, who provided the cover illustration, it wouldn't look as beautiful as it does.

I thank Cathal Larkin, a long-suffering Mayo supporter, for sifting through my work before it went to print.

Finally, I'd like to thank my family – aunts, uncles, cousins, my grandfather; you've all supported me in some way, big or small.

Two of my uncles, tragically, are not here to see this finished product. Tadhgie was killed in 1971, aged just eight, and there's a piece dedicated to him in this book. My uncle, Paddy, died earlier this year, and that has had no small impact on my family. My late grandparents – Kathleen, Bridie, and Pats – also missed out on this day, but they remain very much in my thoughts.

As for my siblings, Bríde and Áine; and my parents – Máire and Pádraig – I would break the word count if I listed every reason I have for thanking them. So, if they don't mind, I'll just settle for 'thank you' – for everything.

Tadhg Evans.

FOREWORD

By Kevin Hughes, Editor of The Kerryman

WATCHING a talent develop, there really is something special about it.

When I first met Tadhg, I found him a determined sort. A college résumé that ticked all the boxes, sample pieces that were text-book perfect and, of course, he talked a good game.

Let's just say I had little hesitation in offering an internship and he duly accepted. I can safely say it was one of the best decisions I've ever made.

From the off, Tadhg handed in a standard of work that impressed hugely. Moreover, in a deadline-driven industry, producing clean, solid copy that is thoroughly researched and backed up by trustworthy sources is a Godsend, and Tadhg did just that.

That's why offering Tadhg a permanent job with *The Kerryman* was a no-brainer, and I've never for one day regretted that decision.

Of course, there were days when things don't go according to plan. It happens. Negative feedback, legitimate or otherwise, that's simply part of a job in which probing questions have to be asked.

At first, Tadhg took things to heart and that's not good for a newspaper journalist. For me, though, it shows compassion, a desire to please. To get to the nub of a story, it's something journalists have to live with, and Tadhg now paddles the choppy waters of our profession with aplomb.

He's most at home, though, with features, interviews and analysis. In fact, he's not just comfortable, he excels in these areas. That's because he has a passion for the subjects of choice.

But much more importantly, he has an inherent empathy with an interviewee that readers can relate to.

I've overheard many of those interviews. In reality, they're not interviews but rather chats. Indeed, all that's missing is the fireplace. That's a skill that, for many, takes years to develop. Tadhg's secret ingredient, though, is hard and extensive preparation before approaching an interviewee.

That's why the countless examples on these pages are simply a pleasure to read. Furthermore, they're easy to read. Interviews move seamlessly from one subject to the next. That doesn't happen by chance; for each interview there are hours and hours of research unbeknownst to the reader.

Of course, there are the funny stories along the way: the cricket interview held for weeks on end due to space issues; the awkward, potentially libellous – and never to be printed – spelling mistakes spotted before *The Kerryman* goes to print; and the stories behind the scenes at Comórtas Peile, where Tadhg can typically be tasked with a 500-word piece yet return with a 2,000-word feature.

And then there are the reasons for those rare mornings when Tadhg may actually be running a little late for work – an exception for a man who can regularly be found in the office before 7am – which inevitably involve some form of livestock on the roads between Lios Póil, Annascaul and Camp. Ever the roving reporter, I'm just waiting for him to interview the farmers in question.

In the following pages the reader will find an eclectic mix of interviews, tales from the four corners of Kerry that will fascinate – from an All-Ireland Hurling Final in Killarney to a former Wexford hurler getting back to basics with the Irish language in west Kerry. Then there are the Dingle men making waves in the US – from starring in Broadway to running across the American continent. And tales, too, from older heads, stories that are worth bottling, such as the memories of the legendary Micheál Ó Muircheartaigh or a century of stories from Beaufort centenarian John Coffey, who sadly passed away just a few months later.

Tadhg Evans

All put together with care and respect for the subject. Quirky, thorough, passionate, industrious, dark-humoured, stripy-jumpered, non-clock-watcher, Gaeilgeoir, GAA man, snooker man, Lios Póil man, West Kerry man: that's our Tadhg.

Kevin Hughes.

Part One

Sport

'I would do anything for that boy'

Mick O'Connell might be the greatest Gaelic Footballer of all time, but he's not the most forthcoming interviewee. That's not an insult; he just doesn't like attention. I knew that before I rang him days after his 80th birthday, and I'd my heart in my mouth before that call. He picked up the phone, called out his number before saying hello – old style – and then I introduced myself and spoke to him in Irish (I'd heard this would be the best way to get him on side). He asked, "Is this going to be printed in Irish or English?"... "In English", I said... "So what's the point in talking to me in Irish?"

I'd been put in my place – but he hadn't said no to an interview.

I always knew this would be the first piece included in this book; it was the first time an article of mine got nationwide traction. I don't think it's anywhere near my best piece – in fact, I've restructured it quite some bit from what appeared in the paper, such is my embarrassment at the way I went about it five years ago – but the public enjoyed it. And you should always give them what they want...

MICK O'Connell saves his strongest words for what matters. The acclaimed Valentian has been called the greatest Gaelic footballer on more than one occasion, but while such praise would rush to most men's heads, O'Connell has always swatted it away like a tennis player serving at match point: "They're only opinions. One man might like my style, but another fella might think it all wrong. I take no notice either way."

Kerry stopped this week to congratulate one of its best footballers on his 80th birthday, but the man himself didn't budge from routine. He walked his dog, stopped at the lighthouse, gazed across at vacant Beginish, and reflected. "Same as I do a lot of days," he says.

It's not false modesty. O'Connell genuinely doesn't think people should idolise him for his near-perfect contribution to a sport he never thought of as more than a pastime. The mention of family, however, prompts a different tone.

After he and Rosaleen married in 1972, the couple had three children: Diarmuid, Máire, and Micheál. Diarmuid, who has Down syndrome, turned 40 last November, and his father describes him as "the greatest gift God ever gave me".

"I would do anything for that boy; he means way more than All-Ireland medals," he says. "People with Down syndrome have lovely, warm personalities. In other parts of the world, they are treated poorly, and that fills me with sadness. But here in Valentia, we have Tigh an Oileáin, and it provides great care to Diarmuid and others – and that makes me happy.

"I allowed Kerry Parents and Friends to use my land for Tigh an Oileáin, but I thought nothing of it. Diarmuid is the greatest gift I ever received, and to see him enjoying himself over there is priceless to me.

"It reminds us how unimportant football is. I learned that while I was growing up. I never treated a win on the football field as a triumph, nor a defeat as a disaster."

O'Connell's name will forever be linked to Gaelic football, but he hasn't allowed the old game to define him. Today, he doesn't even go to see inter-county matches; he views the modern game as a crude imitation of the sport that charmed him in the '40s.

"I call it Gaelic, not Gaelic football. You're only 24, so you wouldn't know anything about the old catch-and-kick style – but it has died out. I go to watch Valentia playing, and that's about it. I don't bother with Kerry games anymore.

"I don't blame the players. The game adapted to the rules that are there. But while I still enjoy watching sport, 'Gaelic' does not hold any appeal to me. It's totally different to the game I used to know."

And home has changed, too. O'Connell grew up in a different Valentia, even learning to play soccer from Spanish boatmen at a time when the island welcomed cable ships from all over the planet:

"Valentia was thriving. Our harbour was going non-stop, and we had every service: schools, a post office, a Garda station, the whole lot. But the cable company closed and everything changed. Like all places on the west, jobs ebbed away, and people moved with them.

"But we're not the only place that suffered. Things change over time. Valentia's different, but that's the way things go."

The Kerryman, January 11, 2017.

A life lived in the fast lane

Paudie Fitzgerald won the 1956 Rás Tailteann – Ireland's best-loved cycle race – and was a businessman of some repute. More importantly, he came from Lios Póil, and that's where this interview took place – in my Granda Tommy's sitting room, to be precise.

Paudie passed away in December of 2020. I'm not sure if anyone else interviewed him after this piece, which ran in 2018, but it was, at the very least, one of the last occasions on which he spoke to a newspaper.

HE was king of Irish cycling. Power and pace made him a contender; dedication made him champion.

But with the Rás Tailteann won, there was nothing left to motivate Paudie Fitzgerald. The raw eggs, drops of sherry, and desire that fuelled his dawn training cycles fell by the wayside, and the heroics dried up. He was great – but he could have been great for longer.

"I won't say I regret it," he shares. "But in later years, I've thought it was a pity nobody told me to stay going. I didn't want to train, and when I was being beaten at sports meetings and road races – I didn't like it."

Over 90 minutes of yarns, Fitzgerald's mischievous smile held true until now. Every previous question drew 20-minute answers, each comic and well told. Seated on a brown leather sofa in my granda Tommy's sitting-room, he's as relaxed as he'd be in his Tralee home. Fitzgerald is at his jovial best sitting across from my grandfather; they've been friends since their Lios Póil childhoods.

"I used to drive around the county, following his cycles," granda says. "One day, I met Gene Mangan stretched in a dyke out by the hills near Tralee. He was exhausted – but he had his own followers to see after him. It was every man for himself!"

Mangan's win in 1955 sparked a golden Rás era for Kerry; after Fitzgerald won in '56, Mick Murphy became champion two years later. But while individual success was sweet, it was of secondary importance.

"It was all about Kerry," Fitzgerald says. "There was fierce rivalry between the counties – especially Kerry and Dublin – and we dominated. One year, Kerry won 34 trophies between the main prizes and the local Rás primes. The presentations were in Dublin afterwards, and we brought cups home in bags."

It was a different time. Just 34 riders opposed Fitzgerald in 1956. Last Sunday, 155 men rolled out of Drogheda for the opening stage of 2018's Rás. Local clubs have more registered members today than the whole of Ireland had when Fitzgerald was the pacesetter.

It's the most noticeable change in Irish cycling, he says, and one he describes as brilliant. But as he talks us through his development from a boy who cycled a 'high nelly' alongside his sister, Hannie Jo, to becoming a core member of Kerry's team aboard a Bianchi – the brand favoured by his idol, Fausto Coppi – his yarns of yesteryear seem a world removed from life today. Every story, right down to his account of the bizarre prizes he won, tells of a changed Ireland and a changed sport.

"We used to have local races; you know the way young fellas challenge each other, 'I'm faster than you', that carry on," he says. "I remember one of the first races I won was back to Dingle, beating Johnny Moriarty. I won a holdall, and I was delighted bringing it home to my mother.

"I won a cycle another time from Ballyferriter to Carrig. Fellas were saying they'd have won only they fell in a pileup – but I avoided it because I went to Keane's for a pint.

"Even the first big race I won – a coast-to-coast from Dublin to Galway and back again – I won a battery for a flash-lamp. 'Eveready' was one of the sponsors, and they gave us a box to share out. They were different times."

Leaving batteries and bags aside, there was no dearth of more traditional prizes. Scores of trophies and cups adorned a sideboard in his mother's house, and children would call in after Sunday Mass for a gawk. It was when a local runner by the name of John Bowler organised a team to tour Kerry's sports meetings that such success became possible. Fitzgerald was a star but not a lone ranger. It was impressive enough that Lios Póil possessed a top cyclist, but Bowler was similarly formidable in his own field, and their respective talents sparked a friendship.

"Bowler broke the four-minute mile ever before Roger Bannister did," Fitzgerald claims, slapping the knees of his white slacks. "I borrowed a yard-measure from my mother and marked out a mile in Gualainn. I brought my two-bell alarm clock one evening and timed him myself.

"We'd cycle to Tralee, stay in Ashe Street overnight, and have our few pints. We'd go to sports meetings then the day after."

Fitzgerald's flair caught the eyes of the county team, and over some three years, his training raised more and more local eyebrows. His mother would prepare porridge and a raw egg for him each morning; once she'd thrown in a squirt of sherry, her boy was ready for road. Before and after a day's labouring, he'd do some 40 miles along the Conor Pass, Slea Head, or wherever took his fancy. His home had no running water, but he was one of the lucky ones; living next to the Abhainn an Londraigh river, freshening up was no bother.

With toil came improvement, and but for misfortune, he could've been champion sooner. His 1954 hopes died in Dublin after getting tangled in tram tracks, but camaraderie had its day; Gene Mangan waited for his colleague – though Mangan said this was at the Lios Póil man's insistence.

But Fitzgerald repaid his debt one year later. Though second in classification when leaving Sligo, another crash delayed the Lios Póil man's destiny by a further year – but he cycled through injury and dejection to complete the Rás and help Mangan to glory.

As far as winning the big one was concerned, it was a case of when, not if, Fitzgerald would reach the pinnacle. His breakthrough finally came in 1956 by way of a Rás with every trait of a 'Wacky Races' episode – but having trained like an Olympian, the aesthetics of his triumph were of no concern to him.

"There was trouble in Cookstown," he says. "One of our cars was carrying a tricolour, and the RUC stopped us. We refused to remove it, so the Orange Order came out and started throwing stones and bottles at us. They stuck pins in our tyres. We abandoned the stage.

"I won both the stage into Tralee and the King of the Mountains on the Ring of Kerry. I'd worked with Galway's Johnny Keane, but there was a timing error, and he was put 20 seconds ahead of me.

"The next stage was to Clonmel. We weren't long out of Kenmare when a group of us took off. By the time I got to Mallow, I was on my own, a good six minutes ahead of the bunch. But outside Mallow, I took a wrong turn towards Mitchelstown and lost more than a minute. I took another wrong turn in Fermoy, and the bunch caught me; Keane was amongst them. He started teasing me, and we came to blows in the middle of a road.

"After we were separated, we went on to Mitchel-stown, where we were held up by a Funeral. I tore up alongside it. Johnny Landers and Stephen Ryan, friends of mine, 'worked' with Keane and pretended to chase me – but they actually slowed the pace, and it took Keane too long to twig it. I thank them very much for it! I was into Clonmel six minutes ahead of Keane. The last stage to Dublin was the easy bit!"

His cheeky smile broadens enough to remind one he's a maverick, a man who left for the Melbourne Olympics knowing he could be thrown out for being selected by the unrecognised 32-county NCA. In being whisked away by police, he delayed the race and made headlines world-wide, but hours after being taken into custody, he found himself dining in the home of the sympathetic Sergeant Cronin. Even in heartache, yarns were in rich supply.

Though unconvincing in denying that he regrets what followed 1956, he has enough to be proud of, and his passion for cycling endures. Today he's looking for-ward to getting home to watch the Giro d'Italia and Sam Bennett – "who'd remind you of nobody only Mangan" – and he spent Friday evening in Manor West with the Kerry team ahead of the Rás. He'll light a few candles for them in Curraheen Church as they take on 'the big one'.

But he speaks of family with a fondness even his cy-cling days can't rival.

His wife, Eileen, died 31 years ago, but the couple had seven children. Fitzgerald remarried; what started with changing a tyre for a lady called Joan on the way to Dublin led to dinner in the Green Isle Hotel. The rest is happy history.

"I'm proud of my family and my grandchildren," he says. "When it comes to sport, Darragh [Fitzgerald] is with Munster rugby, and I've another fella, Gavin Jones, who's in with Leinster.

"You've Paul [Geaney] as well, dad to my 14-month-old great-grandson, Páidí. Paul and Siún, Páidí [Ó] Sé's daughter, are getting married in December, I'm told.

"I remember when Paul was first going to Croke Park, he asked, 'Granda: have you any words of advice?' I threw my arm around him and said, 'Paul, just remember – you're the grandson of the great Paudie Fitzgerald'.

"Anyway, when he won the All-Ireland in 2014, he met me afterwards and got his own back. 'Granda,' he said, 'just remember – you're the grandfather of the great Paul Geaney'."

The Kerryman, May 23, 2018.

Half-ton of gold for Glenbeigh star

I'd never heard of Dominick Lynch until I was scrolling through The Kerryman notes pages one afternoon, looking for potential stories. Under the Glenbeigh section, the notes writer was congratulating some fella on his 50th Munster handball medal, and I assumed it was a misprint.

But my editor, Kevin Hughes, assured me that it wasn't a typo – and then I had to interview the man. How could someone play for that long, let alone be good enough to win?

WHEN a handballer embarks on the long, gnarled bóithrín to greatness, the first trait they must exercise is patience.

Handball requires agility, power, precision, and vision, and its alleys have a knack for tripping even natural athletes; the rubber ball streaks around the court like a stray bullet in a Wild West shootout, often reducing novice players to looking like a disoriented family chasing a bluebottle.

Most tire of the embarrassment and learn to abscond at the sound of squeaking runners and rattling rubber, but some wait and become great.

More than three decades on from serving his handball apprenticeship, Dominick Lynch still 'tips around' the nation's alleys.

It was in Glenbeigh, his home court, that Lynch hoovered up his 50th Munster gold medal on Monday night; a commanding performance in a deciding set condemned Clare's Colin O'Riordan to silver. Lynch, a five-time World Champion, wobbled in the second frame, surrendering a lead when only four points from the title – but rather than indulging panic, the instincts that have helped him to 24 All-Ireland Championships surfaced.

"I thought I'd push on at 17-16 in the second [set], but I left him back into it," he says. "I said I'd slow my serve down for the decider to try and catch him out, and it worked, in fairness…I raced to 10-0, and I knew I had him rattled then."

His boundless ambition first made itself known before his 10th birthday, prompting observers to tell young Lynch he was "going places", and though his teenage years were but a speck in the distance, that Glenbeigh boy knew what he wanted his future to hold.

"My dream was to play in Croke Park, and I realised at a young age that my best chance of doing that would be through handball," he says. "I wanted an All-Ireland badly, and by the time I was playing under-16, I'd done it; John Joe Quirke and myself won the 40x20 All-Ireland Doubles Championship in 1993, so I ticked that box fairly quickly.

"A year later, I won the under-17 40x20 singles at the World Championships in Clare, so then I had to set new targets for myself. At one stage, I wanted to get to 10 Munsters and five All-Irelands, and then it went up to around 30 Munsters and 10 All-Irelands. Now, I have 50 provincial titles, and I'd like to get the 25th All-Ireland soon, all going well!"

Whether it's 40x20, 60x30, singles, doubles, teams, or hardball, Lynch will play. A combination of fluency in all these codes and intense hunger for success fuels the Glenbeigh man, and he's confident that both he and his local football team, preparing for an All-Ireland Junior Championship final, will do 'gaisce' over the coming days.

"The lads [Glenbeigh/Glencar] can win the football next week, and I'd like to think I can back up my win on Monday with the All-Ireland in March," he says with the confidence you'd expect from a 24-time national champion.

The Kerryman, February 15, 2017.

Footnote: Glenbeigh/Glencar did win the All-Ireland a few days later. So did Dominick.

There's much more to Pobalscoil Chorca Dhuibhne than *just* two Hogan Cup titles.

I was in Third Year when Pobalscoil Chorca Dhuibhne opened, and I sat my Leaving in 2011. With typically lousy timing, I was gone just before the school enjoyed its greatest football successes – not that I'd have been playing or anything.

I've never cried after a football match, but the closest I came to that was when the Pobalscoil – 'my' school – won the 2014 Hogan Cup. To be asked a few years later by our Sports Editor, Paul Brennan, to document the Pobalscoil's sporting history ahead of a Munster final was only a pleasure.

COMPILING a concise account of Pobalscoil Chorca Dhuibhne's football history is made tougher by the urge to note the highlights and jump to conclusions – the most tempting of which is to overlook the bulk of its achievements in favour of its two Hogan Cups.

Just 11 years ago, the final pupil took the sharp left coming from CBS Daingean Uí Chúis' front yard, becoming the last of thousands of grey-uniformed boys to descend the Barrack Height. In 2007, the CBS and its equivalent for girls, Meánscoil na Toirbhirte, amalgamated and resettled to a perch on the fringe of The Grove – and, just 12 months later, the eldest of the peninsula's first Hogan Cup-winning players enrolled.

Framed, enlarged versions of *The Kerryman*'s reports on the school's two Hogan Cup wins cling to the sky-blue walls inside the doorway and immediately remind one of the school's greatest footballing days. But before it even won the first of those back-to-back titles, the Pobalscoil had achieved three Corn Uí Mhuirí Munster championships – and even accounting for just senior successes would be tantamount to ignoring a crucial subplot.

Those All-Ireland wins were the apexes of a dynasty – but the school's most intimidating show of strength arrived in 2011/12, when it razed opposition of all ages in Kerry and Munster to return six championships. It's telling in itself that Matthew Flaherty, speaking to *The Kerryman* today, wasn't unique in winning 10 major trophies during his schooldays – and, just as it would be a disservice to refer to Flaherty as merely a one-time Hogan Cup winner, Principal Padraig Feirtéir feels it would be unfair to look at the Pobalscoil's two All-Irelands and ignore its other triumphs, many of which were secured by boys and girls away from football fields.

"I can't say how appreciative I am that our teachers put in so much time with extra-curricular activities,"

Feirtéir says. "They do that of their own free will, against all the extra demands that come with being a teacher nowadays."

Both Flaherty and Outdoor Sports Co-ordinator Tomás Mac Cárthaigh echo that point. The school loses little energy beyond 4pm as students branch from class-rooms to whatever activities are billed for the evening – and Flaherty counts himself as one of hundreds who've gained from the Pobalscoil's commitment to extra-curricular interests.

"The school had a lot to do with it," he says. "Even when we were in Second Year, on the back field of the old CBS pitch ahead of a Russell Cup game, Éamonn [Fitzmaurice] mentioned the Hogan Cup and Corn Uí Mhuirí to us.

"We were only 14, and it dawned on us what he had said. We were taken aback that he was talking about this and that he believed, even then, that we could win them.

"That stayed with us right until the Hogan Cup final in 2014, when we were well behind against Maghera at half-time. We took a breather and let Éamonn speak, and he told us it was our last 30 minutes together – ever.

"I distinctly remember there was a map of Ireland in the dressing room, and Éamonn brought us into a huddle, pointed at the map, and said: 'when we finish this game, we'll be kingpins of this country'. We were men possessed in the second half. It was something Éamonn, Seán Ó Dálaigh, Tomás Ó Beaglaíoch, Tommy Griffin, and the likes had instilled in us throughout the years.

"It's the best thing I've won to date. Winning an All-Ireland Minor medal with Kerry was great, but winning with my best friends, fellas I sat next to for six years, having the craic with at lunchtime – you can't beat that. Having the likes of Cian Murphy and Tadhgie Browne running towards me after the final whistle was unbelievable."

In Flaherty and MacCárthaigh's views, that win was a product not only of coaching and talent but also of an unsung school tradition, and structures within local football.

Dingle and An Ghaeltacht's seniors have since re-established themselves as two of Kerry's premier outfits. Lios Póil has risen to Division Three and captured its first Munster Novice Championship in 2017. Annascaul lads were crucial to the school's Under-16-and-a-half All-Ireland-winning panel of 2017, and their influence has been felt as keenly in the build-up to Saturday's final.

On tradition, Flaherty, for all his youth, asserts that memories of the late Liam Higgins – who was a mastermind contributor to the old CBS's successes, namely the All-Ireland B Championship-winning years of 1995 and 2001 – were never far removed from the minds of the mentors who guided him during his schooldays.

Mac Cárthaigh has lent his support ever since joining the CBS's staff almost a quarter of a century ago and recognises that the recent successes grew from a place that far predates the school's 2007 opening day – but he's more preoccupied with the present and future than the historic texts resting in the Pobalscoil's domed, timber-framed library.

"I've seen it all. I remember the first All-Ireland B Final against Banada Abbey, Sligo, above in Ennis... There's no doubt that our opponents [CBS, The Green] have a great tradition – but we're trying to plough our own."

The Kerryman, February 21, 2018.

Footnote: The Pobalscoil won the Munster final against CBS The Green that year but fell short, sadly, in their All-Ireland semi-final.

Bats, balls, sun, and sandwiches.

Visiting County Kerry Cricket Club's Oyster Oval made for another one of those days when work didn't feel like work. I sat down with a view of Tralee Bay, had a cup of coffee, and chatted to a few fellas who tried to explain the intricacies of a game I know very little about.

THE welcome at The Spa's Oyster Oval is reason enough to call in for an afternoon's cricket. If you add sunshine and the presence of the world-famous Marylebone Cricket Club (MCC), it might even be the perfect alternative to a day's office work.

A Kerry flag and the MCC's red and yellow stripes hang from a practice net and ripple in the sea breeze. With two wickets already captured, County Kerry spinner Kashif Khan skips uphill and bowls to Zimbabwean international PJ Moor. Stepping towards the delivery, Moor swings bat to ball; his technique and timing are spectacles in themselves. Willow cracks against leather; the ball clears the fence and glides to the shoreline.

"Thank God the tide is out," County Kerry Chairman Dave Ramsay quips with a shake of his head. "This guy is murdering us."

When the Zimbabwean came to the crease, the MCC was in a world of trouble at 16 for three; since Moor fastened his bottle-green helmet, he and Fiachra Tucker have combined for 53 runs.

They'll add plenty more – but they won't quench home spirits.

We're many miles from the Caribbean or Karachi, but while Kerry's cricket history is lean relative to the standards of those heartlands, it's neither short nor insignificant.

County Kerry Cricket Club came into some form of existence in 1872 when players padded up at the Military Barracks in Ballymullen. Indeed, the sound of leather on willow was familiar to many parts of the county until the mid-20th century.

"It was quite a big game in Kerry," Joe Revington says from a plastic chair on the pavilion's timber decking. "But it kind of died in Wartime and became a banned game.

"It wasn't immediately banned; they played for many years at the barracks and places such as Waterville and Valentia. There was a lot of cricket here."

Its decline in Kerry seemed irreversible for much of the 20th century – but cricket reignited here in the late 1980s, Ramsay says, when Tralee Rugby Club's Eric Lye asked teammates if they fancied a game.

"I went to school in Gonzaga College, Dublin, where cricket was a big thing, so that's how I got into it," Ramsay says. "Since 1988, we've come a long way. Today, we effectively have four teams and 50 playing members, from the Munster Premier Division down to Division Three.

"We also play in the Munster Senior, Junior, and Minor Cups. We've made the quarter-finals of the National Cup for the last two years, and we're playing against DLR, an amalgamation of south County Dublin teams, in the second round on June 17.

"We've some nice players. Yaqoob Ali is our senior captain. He played with Ireland 'A' and represents Munster in the inter-pros. He recently took four international wickets against Leinster. If you look elsewhere, Usman [Khan] has started the season well with bat and ball. The quality is there."

At Ramsay's mention of quality, Moor offers another glimpse of his talent. In pushing away a Kashif delivery, he connects with the ball's sweet spot; it rolls, like a tumbleweed, to the boundary rope.

His partnership with Tucker has long raced past 50 runs and soothed any early worries for the world's best-known club. 230 years on from its foundation, the MCC has 23,500 members, and they own Lord's Cricket Ground and its assets. With roughly 2,000 playing members to choose from, it despatches teams to venues throughout the UK and overseas to fulfil some 500 matches annually.

"We gauge the opposition and line out based on their ability," says the MCC's Peter MacDonald, who has joined Ramsay for a natter by a picnic table. "The ideal scenario is to give the supporters a decent game; we're about developing cricket.

"PJ, over there, has played for Zimbabwe at the highest level. But you'd have a lot of guys out there who'd have never met each other before today – and that's quite common for us.

"We played here last year at the official opening. It went well, so we said we'd do it again. And when you get to look out at that bay – it's stunning, just stunning."

Finding a home for the club realised a long-held ambition for Ramsay – but to acquire a ground of this beauty would have been beyond even his most vivid dreams. The club's more nomadic days saw them wander from one temporary shelter to another; before acquiring the Oyster Oval, players kitted out at the Tralee Sports Complex.

But for all the progress and idyllic scenery, Tralee Bay has seen cloudy days and will encounter more – unimaginable though they may be on a day as sunny and spirited as today.

"We've lost our local Twenty20 league," Ramsay says. "Dingle had a very handy side; they had about five Aussies who came over during the boom. Killarney and Tralee had some good teams. But the recession bit hard, and a lot of clubs couldn't keep it up.

"It could start again. Killarney is a sleeping giant; they have a significant population of Bangladeshis and others of Asian descent. The main problem is we don't have the qualified personnel to go into schools.

"We do junior cricket, but you need two or three people to oversee it. You have to be interested in doing it in the first place. Secondly, you need to be Garda-vetted. It's very difficult when you're reliant on volunteers."

Several members express similar opinions throughout the afternoon. The club has a large number of Asian players, but while their importance is undoubted, there's no sense amongst the patrons that Kerry is overly dependent on them. That's not the main conundrum.

"We've a wide range of nationalities involved, and there are Irish players coming on stream," vice-chairman Richard Rutland explains. "We have a former Kerry hurler, Ian Brick, for example. He's not at the top level yet, but he got into it through playing Twenty20, and he's been with us for five or six years now. His son, Jordan, and brother, David, have also been involved.

"Youth is a problem. We had a team from Valentia who would travel here every week, religiously, but they were an ageing outfit and couldn't keep it up – and that wasn't an issue confined to them."

At the highest level, cricket authorities take a snootier attitude than most to emerging nations. Ireland recently became just the 11th nation to acquire Test status, and this was after more than a decade of decking giants such as England, Pakistan, and the West Indies on the One-Day scene.

Test cricket, played over five days, is the game in its purest and most brutal form. New Zealand had to wait 26 years for its first win, and only Australia won its first test. Almost 150 years later, Ireland nearly emulated 'the baggy greens'; but for a fifth-day revival, Ireland's opponent, Pakistan, would have left Malahide to humiliation.

While Test status comes with financial gain – some 20 million people in Pakistan watched the Malahide test, thus generating massive revenue – Ramsay is sceptical that it will inspire Ireland's youth at grassroots level.

The Test game unwinds too gradually for an era of dwindling attention spans, and without free-to-air TV coverage, it's hard to see how youngsters will fall for its ways.

Since Sky acquired the rights to England Tests, the five-day game's exposure has nosedived in the UK. A 2016 poll found that more English children recognised wrestler John Cena, the star of a scripted sport, than the legendary Alastair Cook.

"Tests are important from an economic point of view and holding on to our top internationals, but when it comes to attracting youngsters – I don't know," Ramsay says, as agitated by the mound of sandwiches left over in the pavilion as he is at Moor, who has just cannoned another ball to the shoreline.

"Not qualifying for the World Cup was a bigger deal because it would've been on in the UK, right next door. We messed up in the qualifiers in Zimbabwe, and it was a bloody poor effort if you ask me.

"I'd fancy Kerry to be stronger if we get into the schools – but that's an ongoing saga."

The Kerryman, June 6, 2018.

Footnote: Moor topped the scoresheet with 86. At the close of play, Kerry trailed by 77 runs in reply to the MCC's 225 – but the MCC failed to bowl Kerry out, resulting in a drawn match.

Killarney's hurling showpiece.

Every day's a school day in journalism. I thought Kevin Hughes was having me on when he told me Killarney had hosted an All-Ireland Hurling Final. Thankfully he had a number for sports historian Richard McElligott to confirm his claim, or I'd have never believed it.

It happened all right, in 1937. It was a Tipp–Kilkenny final; at least that much was believable.

IT'S the most surprising of historical snippets. The mere sight of a sliotar, of all things, darting through the sky over Fitzgerald Stadium would be a happening rare enough to put bumps on the pulse of the most relaxed GAA man.

But according to those in the know, the surprise caused by billing an All-Ireland Senior Hurling Final, the sport's biggest game, for Fitzgerald Stadium, the darling of Lewis Road, was not nearly as sharp as one might assume.

"Given everything that happened during 1937, Killarney actually became the logical choice to host that year's All-Ireland Hurling Final," UCD Lecturer in Modern Irish History Richard McElligott explains to *The Kerryman*, precisely 80 years on from the biggest sporting spectacle ever to enter the kingdom.

"Just weeks after the iconic Dick Fitzgerald's passing in September 1930, a Dr Crokes meeting prompted efforts to build a new stadium in tribute to Kerry GAA's first superstar. Some six years of work culminated in the opening of Fitzgerald Stadium in 1936, the country's second-largest venue and a project typical of a time of expansion for the association. Thousands had started going to matches all over the country by then, and even Croke Park was struggling to meet the public's appetite – and this would lead to a sooner-than-expected day in the sun for Killarney's new venue.

"In February 1936, redevelopment began on the Cusack Stand and Hill 16, and the finished product was meant to come on stream in August 1937, just in time for the All-Ireland finals. But a massive strike broke out between Dublin's builders and the Irish Free State Federation of Building Contractors, and demands for a weekly pay rise of 11 shillings curbed all construction in the city. With the hurling final drawing closer, it became apparent that Croke Park wouldn't be ready for the hurling All-Ireland, so the GAA looked elsewhere – and Killarney's new masterpiece came into view."

With redevelopments also at a sensitive point in the home of hurling, Thurles' Semple Stadium, a coupling of odd circumstances and Killarney's impressive facilities made the Kerry town the only candidate with the muscle to support the year's biggest match.

Ahead of the final, Central Council gave Killarney unanimous backing, and hurling's premier occasion was destined for temporary shelter within football's leafiest forest.

"It might seem strange today that it was billed for Kerry and a ground that is now so heavily associated with football, but Fitzgerald Stadium had only narrowly missed out on hosting the Munster Hurling Final in 1937, and Dr Eamonn O'Sullivan had never intended for the pitch to serve just one code," says Richard.

"Even though there was a weaker hurling tradition in Kerry than in other counties, the locals were delighted at the news from GAA headquarters. Just one year previously, Killarney successfully hosted an Irish Eucharistic Congress, and its reputation for tourism was beginning to blossom.

"*The Kerryman* summed up the county's mood at the time of the GAA's decision, lauding it as recognition of both a great town and a great stadium. While hurling wasn't Kerry's game, the county very much embraced the hurling final."

More than 25 specially commissioned trains from all over the county and country chugged through the town bounds for the clash of arch-rivals Tipperary and Kilkenny and, by the eve of the final, a tide of thousands of people had overwhelmed Killarney's accommodation resources.

The crowd enveloping Killarney's streets offered a sample of each of the country's accents, and as Saturday night gave way to the dawn of All-Ireland Sunday, the people of Kerry leapt into an unprecedented and unrepeated celebration.

"Over 43,000 attended – a record for Fitzgerald Stadium that stood until the Kerry-Cork Munster football semi-final of 1998 – and it was far from just Kilkenny and Tipperary folk that crossed the county bounds," Richard says. "Back then, All-Irelands were All-Irelands in every sense of the term, and you had people from Derry, Belfast, Dublin, and goodness knows where else down to make a weekend of it.

"On Sunday morning, hundreds of cars and dozens of buses rolled in – an extraordinary sight for a time of little motor activity – and for the first time, Killarney saw fields used as car parks, with frustrated drivers abandoning their motors in exasperation at the lack of parking.

"The whole of Kerry embraced the day. One of the great quotes from the time claimed there were no men left on the Blaskets that Sunday; they all rowed to the mainland for the match. It was a wonderful occasion."

Before the game, Tipperary captain Jimmy Lannigan gave a cocksure interview worlds removed from the non-views routinely shared by today's more reserved stars. Lannigan's team had just toppled Mick Mackey's mighty Limerick in the Munster final, and this was reason enough to launch the Premier County to undisputed Championship favouritism.

Tipperary's opponent was a fading Kilkenny, which had slinked its way to the decider by way of uninspiring wins over Westmeath and Galway. So Lannigan's confidence, while grating, seemed well placed. So it proved.

"Whatever about the occasion, the match was a disaster," Richard says. "Once the Bishop of Ossory threw the ball in, everything gave way to the inevitable. Kilkenny threw the great Lory Meagher on with some 20 minutes gone, but that proved to be one of the game's few talking points.

"Tipp had two goals on the board by then, and the game was as good as over. It ultimately finished 3-11 to 0-3, and it's still regarded as one of the worst finals."

Altogether more interesting than the match itself is the examination of its legacy. While the occasion proved Killarney could host big games, the town didn't host a Munster Hurling Final until 1950 as provincial council ignored Kerry in favour of Limerick and Thurles. By the 1950s, Dr O'Sullivan lamented that the stadium had become something of a white elephant, caged and unable to reach its potential.

"Once Páirc Uí Chaoimh came on stream, Killarney fell further down the order," Richard says. "The stadium hasn't hosted any inter-county hurling game since the 2004 qualifier between Tipperary and Cork, and that famine is unlikely to end any time soon. Regarding the sport itself, hurling people hoped the final would stimulate interest in the game in south Kerry but, as I'm sure you already know, this hope also faded to nothing.

"What can be said about the 1937 final is that it was a unique occasion. It was an honour to Dick Fitzgerald and a hat-tip to the phenomenal work of people like Dr Eamon O'Sullivan, and while it [Killarney] never took off as a hurling venue, Fitzgerald Stadium has at least become a Cathedral of football since.

"Today, it's my favourite place to watch football. There's nothing better than looking out towards MacGillicuddy's Reeks while you're beating Cork under the summer sunshine – and long may days like those continue!"

The Kerryman, September 6, 2017.

'Give everything a chance.'

I can't remember when I first thought of interviewing GAA commentator Micheál Ó Muircheartaigh, but it was long before I did so in summer 2018. I'd spoken to him a few times on the phone but finally got my chance to sit down with him two years after I'd started with The Kerryman.

I'll have to thank my aunt, Áine, for that one; she's married to his nephew. Handy.

IT'S no short walk from Dún Síon to Dingle town – roughly half an hour to 40 minutes, Micheál Ó Muircheartaigh says.

Men half his age might hide from such exercise, but there isn't a stray puff from the 87-year-old as he surveys a handsome lounge at the back of Dingle Benners Hotel. The room glows in the Friday-afternoon sunshine filtering in, and everything from the brown leather furniture, mahogany coffee table, and electric stove come under Ó Muircheartaigh's inspection.

Perhaps the most impressive feature is a grand bookshelf holding editions of 'Encyclopedia Britannica'. One wonders if they contain anything Ó Muircheartaigh doesn't already know.

"There's something very nice about those old black and white pictures," he says as he continues exploring. "Wouldn't it be nice to know who they all were?"

This thirst for detail marked him as unique amongst his peers. Whereas other commentators told us what was happening, Ó Muircheartaigh did all that and gave us extracts from his subjects' life stories for added value.

When I decided on a career in media, I felt a word of his advice would be worth more than an essay from others. With his nephew wed to my aunt, my chance was as good as readymade.

It came as surprising when my aunt arrived back with his message that being controversial is good if you want to 'make it'. The classic Ó Muircheartaigh commentary was colourful and passionate, funny and informative – but never divisive.

I quote his line back to him as a waitress leaves a pot of tea on the table beside us – but he adds an important detail: "Being controversial is fine – but there must be substance to it".

"In other words, there's another view to everything," he says. "But I always believe that, whatever you're doing, you should be fair to people.

"The guy who used to do rugby commentary for the BBC, Bill McLaren, used to listen back on his broadcasts to see if he was fair to everyone. That was his motto – and it was a good way to be."

It was one of the few aspects of Ó Muircheartaigh's career that remained present from start to finish.

For 61 years, he was the effective owner of the crow's nest in Croke Park. His stretch began after spotting a notice in St Patrick's College advertising commentary trials ahead of the 1949 Railway Cup decider, and it ended in 2010, shortly after he announced Cork as All-Ireland football champions. In the interim, change was constant.

While Paddy O'Keeffe was Director General, Ó Muircheartaigh and his peers were warned not to comment if anyone was injured, in case those listening might get worried. Letting the nation know that someone was sent off was an even more grave offence. Television, naturally, put paid to such nonsense.

And that's just one change.

"I remember it was tried by Raidió Éireann in the early 1950s to make the first attempt at interviewing players; that was with the great Cork hurling team of that time," he recalls. "The interviewer had met the players beforehand and found them fine, friendly. But the moment he produced his recorder, he was on his own inside two minutes. They all had 'something urgent' to see to.

"You could go into a secondary school now with a junior team, and they'd handle any situation. Some teams nowadays might dodge questions – but they're available.

"Everything changes – and I always believe it's a bad outlook to be against change. The first radio station in

Ireland had only been in existence for eight months of 1926 when one of its employees went to Croke Park and told them he had equipment for a man to talk over that Sunday's hurling semi-final between Galway and Kilkenny. It was the first live sports broadcast anywhere in the world – and look what that grew into.

"That came from an idea. The All-Ireland championships themselves started with an idea. Like the 'Super Eights' in football, some people were against it. But I say: give everything a chance. It's not the end of the world if you fail; it's not a crime to fail."

Not all change is positive, though. Or, to be more precise, some changes are more open to questioning. Ó Muircheartaigh's career lived through most watershed moments in GAA broadcasting – but one of the most divisive arrived some four years after his retirement.

The 2014 championship meeting of Kilkenny and Offaly should have never been memorable, ending as it did with the cats' 26-point mauling of the faithful county. But in being beamed by Sky Sports, it was the association's first move away from terrestrial coverage.

The topic is as raw now as it was then, and Ó Muircheartaigh has much company in remaining unconvinced. As a regular visitor to the Asian Gaelic Games, he knows the value of giving the GAA community abroad its opportunity to watch – but his stand remains the same: "All games should be available to the national broadcaster... and let whoever else wants it have it as well".

Some say decisions such as those leading to the Sky deal are signs that GAA headquarters has lost its common touch, though Ó Muircheartaigh doesn't subscribe to that line. Most of those 'elites' consist of ordinary club people from every part of Ireland, he points out.

What's not debatable is that it's been a rough summer for the association, which sustained white-hot criticism in debates over 'Newbridge or nowhere' and the Liam Miller tribute match.

On 'Newbridge or nowhere', Ó Muircheartaigh says Kildare folk were entitled to feel aggrieved when organisers initially billed their qualifier for Croke Park in spite of 'The Lilywhites' being entitled to home advantage. The GAA's handling of the Liam Miller game, in his view, was another misstep.

"A good turn creates goodwill," he says. "The greatest flood of goodwill the GAA got was when they opened Croke Park to rugby and soccer.

"I know the clause was there that Páirc Uí Chaoimh couldn't be used as the rules stood. But it isn't really a game. Nothing depends on the result. Nothing depends on the goals or the wides. There won't be controversy. Liam had played hurling himself and I'm sure always took an interest in it.

"Maybe the situation was handled badly – but they came to the right decision in the end, and it will be forgotten about quickly as well. One or two good games will always kill topics like that."

But while this summer was as rich in controversy as it was sunshine, good games were as sparse as rainfall, at least where football was concerned. Though the hurling was almost surreal in its drama, the football felt as engaging as a Fair City rerun.

Extending each half by five minutes could induce tired mistakes – and with it, excitement – from teams programmed for little more than containment, Ó Muircheartaigh says, and forcing goalkeepers to send kickouts beyond their '45' might lessen hand-passing between defenders.

Whatever the solution, when the voice of the sport says his game is flagging, the public's concerns feel more serious.

"I don't have the answer, but it's not as enjoyable as it used to be," Ó Muircheartaigh admits. "It's no longer about how our full back will hold their full forward; players find themselves in strange parts of the field at any one time. I think that not having those match-ups takes away some of the magic. There's no entertainment in watching a team passing the ball back and across.

"I remember when rugby was a terribly dull game. Many international games finished three points to six, usually all frees. But there was a meeting in the 1990s between the countries that play at a high level, and the agenda was how to make rugby more attractive to spectators. I thought that was a brilliant idea, and it is certainly more entertaining since they developed the rules.

"You see the hurlers this year, they went out to win. Some of the football teams just went out to contain the other team. I know a football manager, I won't name him, and he said, 'We're not there to entertain'. I don't think you can dismiss any element: managers, selectors, or anything. But you certainly can't dismiss the supporters – and they come for entertainment."

Confessions made, he slopes back on a tartan-clad sofa and closes his flip phone; arrangements are in place for one of his "crowd" to spin him back to Dún Síon.

It's two hours since he walked into Benners when, save for the usual greetings, his first words were of his deep respect for his townland's Camphill Community, which works for people with intellectual disabilities and other special needs. Those of us who love sport are often guilty of treating it as more than the triviality it is, but the important stuff lies elsewhere.

Also a member of the IT Tralee Foundation Board and the efforts to complete the €16.5million Kerry Sports Academy, Ó Muircheartaigh said one of that project's goals – to cater for those with disabilities – was something he found most attractive.

"When I was told what it would contain, what appealed to me was that the facilities would be for people with any disability, as well as the elite," he says. "In addition to that, there would be a course in the college, catering for people with disabilities. I said I'd go on the board then.

"It was someone else's idea to have a gala night on September 22 at the Clayton Burlington Hotel with my name associated. The takings, which will be substantial, will all go to the IT. There's a lot of support for this project all over the country, and we didn't just want this to be a local thing; this is a national principle.

"I'm attached to the Special Olympics with a number of years, and it's fantastic, of great value to people. They're growing all the time across the country; parents, friends, and communities are all behind that.

"When the World Games were held in Ireland, it was a massive success. But the real test was afterwards; when you hit a peak, usually, the number of clubs drops off. The exact opposite happened here – and isn't that wonderful?"

The Kerryman, August 15, 2018.
The Corkman, August 23, 2018.

'This isn't a threat... this is about survival.'

Valentia folk were petrified that 2019 would be the year they'd finally be left without a football team. After many years struggling for numbers, the club finally appeared to be doomed. Their season – and perhaps their future – depended on a motion they had prepared for the then-upcoming GAA Congress in Wexford.

The club's Chairperson, Deirdre Lyne, was only too willing to speak to me in Killarney a couple of weeks ahead of the season, and she described, very plainly, what her community was facing.

EVENTS at last December's South Kerry Final could've passed for scripted drama.

Neither the game nor its result were cause for excitement unless you have an attachment to St Marys; Cahersiveen finished 11 points clear of Dromid Pearses and retained a title the club has held since 2014.

The day's subplots trumped the main storyline: Bryan Sheehan gave a man-of-the-match display to complement his achievement of equalling Austin Constable's record of 11 championship medals as he and his team played their way to a rare divisional five-in-a-row.

But perhaps the most remarkable of the day's happenings was the 25-year commemoration of Valentia Young Islanders' 1993 championship-winning team.

Such celebrations are a fixture of major final days, but to have four on a jubilee team – three aged over 40 and one over 50 – still togging out for senior football today was surely unique. The eldest of the quartet, 52-year-old goalkeeper Richard Quigley, even played against his son when Valentia fell to 'Marys' at the semi-final stage.

Everyone who follows Kerry's club scene knows Valentia struggles for numbers; it's just six years since the club sweated over fielding a senior team at all for 2013. In the end, a team came together to avoid a repeat of 1968, when Valentia was again short of numbers, largely due to the closure of the island's trans-Atlantic cable station.

Last December's commemoration could be taken as a dispiriting sign of the times for a club that has won county competitions at all grades and remains the South Kerry Championship's second-most successful team.

The four elder statesmen – Quigley, John Daly, Junior Murphy, and John Shanahan – have served their club with distinction, however. Chairperson Deirdre Lyne has nothing but praise for their part in keeping the team afloat in 2013 and for staying on board until it returned to relatively good health.

Last year, Valentia had a panel of over 20 players and won promotion to Division Four of the County League. But just three months on from a rare win over Waterville in a South Kerry quarter final, a triumph celebrated as though it were a county title, the club is back on the brink. Just 13 players have declared themselves available with just 18 days to go to a 2019 County League opener against St Michaels/Foilmore.

"We have two going travelling, two with long-term injuries, and a couple of retirements," Deirdre says in Petit Delice, a cosy café not far from her workplace in Killarney.

"We've paid our affiliation for this year, and our insurance is due around March. On paper, we've entered the league and championship. Whether we'll be there come March – I don't know. We've had no new players coming into the squad as 17- or 18-year-olds.

"It's been knocking on the door in south Kerry; all the clubs have gone through amalgamations from under-14 up in the last few years, even St Marys and Renard. Last year we had no minor team, so some of our fellas played with Waterville/Dromid – just to keep Waterville/Dromid alive.

"A few years back, there was even a St Finians team with Sneem, Derrynane, Skellig Rangers, and Valentia together for a 13-a-side minor team. Some people used to call us St Vincent de Paul – but that's what we're up against."

The club's immediate future might depend on a motion it submitted for this weekend's GAA Congress in Wexford. If successful, it will allow counties to set a bye-law whereby a 16-year-old can play non-championship games – if their club has junior status and just one adult team.

There has been much focus on younger players' welfare in recent years – and that's a good thing, naturally. But Deirdre's arguments, to park neutrality for a moment, are interesting: these players would be in their 17th year and surely better suited to senior football than most aged over 40. League, anyway, is generally less intense than championship fare.

If it passes, the club could welcome four new players and a clearer future. But if it can't play in the league, which it won as a Division One team in 1984, some potential is at risk of going unrealised.

Valentia was only four points off Churchill in last year's Division Five final. For context, the improving north Kerry club had just lost by a point after extra time in a County Junior semi-final. Its conqueror, Beaufort, went on to win the All-Ireland.

Islander Brendan O'Sullivan has worn the county jersey at senior level, and his brother, Paul, was an All-Ireland medallist with Kerry's juniors. Perhaps more importantly, it'd be no surprise right now to see 10 Valentians togging out for a Monday-night training session; the club is short of numbers but not quality or commitment.

That Valentia will this year field its own under-14 team for the first time this decade, Deirdre says, is further cause for optimism; if the show continues until some of these youngsters make it to senior, the club could be well set in years to come.

But if there's a blackout, as there was in 1968, it could cost the club some of its fringe players, and youngsters will reach senior as replacements, not additions.

"We put it back to the community at an emergency meeting in January," Deirdre says. "The commitment is there; a few players had planned on retiring but have since cancelled their plans. A few volunteered to try and get more players involved – but that hasn't been successful.

"The motion could be the difference; we have four lads we could bring in. It only applies to the league, but we're okay with missing the Club Championship, which only guarantees you three games; the league guarantees you 11, and it's what you base your year on.

"We want to play in everything, but if we have to forfeit championship to survive – so be it. All our league games, bar two, are either at home, or away to a South Kerry team, so it couldn't have worked out much better. Fellas coming home for matches can stay in Valentia at the weekend, so that should be attractive.

"It's frustrating because, if we can get there, we'll be in a better place come June: we've a fella coming back from Shanghai; another fella had surgery two weeks ago but would be back in June; Brendan [O'Sullivan] could be back mid-summer; and one fella is away for three months but will be back for the summer."

Islanders know that their sod's history is one of undulations, and their GAA team has often reflected goings on around here; today's worries coincide with the island having a population of just 654, its lowest since the Famine.

When the cable station closed in 1966, some 100 people left the island almost overnight and, with it, the club lost footballers, and children who might have gone on to wear the jersey. What followed was the blackout of 1968, and they lost further players, most notably Mick O'Connell, to rival clubs.

The population hasn't fallen much further in the interim, but the average age around here has climbed. That's why 1968 threatens to reappear.

That said, there's a sense here that the cable station, 53 years on from its closure, could prove Valentia's saviour again – and what's good for the island should be good for football.

The cable stretched from Knightstown to Heart's Content, Newfoundland, Canada, and placed Valentia at the heart of global communications for roughly a century.

But rather than resting on this legacy, a foundation board's bid for UNESCO World Heritage Site status for the station has progressed well – and could be worth tens of thousands of visitors annually if successful. The board hopes the site will next advance to the government's Irish tentative list, a required step ahead of UNESCO deciding whether to award the station World Heritage status or not.

Kerry County Council also received €1.27million under the Rural Regeneration and Development Fund last November to help develop a ground-floor museum and interpretive centre at the station, as well as an upstairs innovation hub.

Though the Knightstown building's contents were auctioned off following its 1966 closure, its twin in Newfoundland has plenty of stored equipment to help furnish an accurate cable display in Valentia.

It's one of several green shoots sprouting around Valentia right now, and each is a cause for optimism for the Young Islanders: attractions create jobs, which in turn bring people – and potential new players. The club's immediate focus, however, is on congress and a motion that could ensure league participation and the retention of the players it has, whereas a blackout now could have implications for the bright future planned.

"If you leave our senior team go, you've another heartbeat gone from Valentia," Deirdre says.

"I find it overwhelming at times, but I feel an awful responsibility to keep this club and senior team going.

"I love my life on the island. I commute from there to Killarney every day for work – and I'm more than happy to do it...But if you take the senior team out of Chapeltown – people will drive through. The only thing we have on the island right now is Mass every second Sunday; it doesn't even happen every Sunday.

"This isn't a threat; this club really only has 13 players. This is about survival."

The Kerryman, February 20, 2019.

Footnote: Valentia's motion failed, and while 2019 wasn't a blackout, they forfeited many games in both league and championship that year.

They did well in the South Kerry Championship that winter, falling just short in a semi-final against St Mary's, but in 2021, the club announced that it was looking to partner with another outfit.

They later decided to enter Division Six of the County League.

Ready and set to face the best.

The Special Olympics is a movement I've admired since Ireland hosted the World Games in 2003. Many became volunteers afterwards and continue to volunteer today.

People talk about an Olympic legacy – there you have it.

"LET me win, but if I cannot win, let me be brave in the attempt."

It's difficult to recall how aware the Irish public was of the Special Olympics motto prior to the visit of the World Games to Dublin 15 summers ago – but over the course of those nine days in 2003, it was locked into the nation's psyche and has remained there ever since.

Kerry hosted athletes from throughout Europe and Africa that summer in an arrangement that meant even communities based more than 300 kilometres from the host city could sample the Games' charms.

This writer can still recall his elder schoolmates – sixth-class pupils at Scoil Naomh Eoin Baiste, Lios Póil – falling 0-4 down inside 10 minutes to the visiting South African footballers on a sloped pitch adjacent to the school building. Thinking back, two images remain as fresh now as they were on the day they unfolded: firstly, the occasion's cheer and colour took hold of all our imaginations. The Special Olympics movement announced itself to Lios Póil that day and did likewise in thousands more Irish towns and parishes many weeks before the Olympic flame reached full bloom in Croke Park.

The second memory is of the whirlwind of South African pace and passing; it knocked crack after crack into the opposition defence and could only have been the product of skill mixed with diligent practice. These sportsmen had not merely shown us what people with intellectual disabilities could do; they gave us a sense of the preparation that they, and the coaches behind them, had carried out ahead of the Games.

One can't recall if the South Africans went on to medal later that summer but one can safely assume they were brave in their attempt.

Moving down to Kerry's grassroots ahead of this week's Ireland Games, it seems as though our local athletes, set to represent Team Munster, have also prepared with conviction.

More than 20 kingdom sportspeople will participate in Dublin from tomorrow through to Sunday – but one should keep their many coaches and volunteers in mind when following Team Munster's progress.

"We have four athletes going, and Shane Roach is going as a coach," Tralee Together Special Olympics volunteer Lorna O'Sullivan says. "We started out after the World Games in 2003 after Tralee hosted the El Salvador team. We'd noticed there were no local members on the Irish team. There are eight people on our committee and a host of volunteers – not least from the Tralee schools, who each help us out in six-week blocks."

Lorna, who oversees training at Cumann Iosaef every Saturday, describes Tralee Together as a "marvellous group", and while much of her current excitement derives from the upcoming Games, she is equally buoyant for the torch run through Kerry on Monday and the visit to the county of Timothy Shriver, son of Special Olympics founder Eunice Kennedy Shriver.

Anticipation for the torch run is similarly keen in Kerry's other leading clubs, as is their dedication to the movement. Kerry Stars, covering Killarney and its surrounds, was founded in September 2002 after local families recognised the need for such a club. It has since grown from facilitating 12 athletes in one sport to a wide-ranging movement catering for more than 100 athletes in athletics, swimming, soccer, golf, and basketball.

"We train all year round," vice-chairman Tom Tobin says. "We're at the indoor hall at Spa GAA club every Monday evening, and we move out to An Ríocht when the weather clears up. We added basketball last year at Killarney Sports and Leisure Complex, with much help from Saint Paul's [basketball club], I should add. We also use Killarney Celtic's facilities; Fairways Golf, Kenmare;

the Ross; Tralee Leisure Complex; and the Castlerosse Hotel. The whole thing has just kept growing.

"I was based out of Killarney Garda Station in the Special Olympics year, 2003. Nick Maher was in charge of the volunteering for the Italian team we were hosting, but he was on holidays the week it was on – so I took on that job, and through that, I got to know some of the Kerry Stars.

"The problem with growing in the way we have is that you always need volunteers, but we're very lucky in Killarney in that regard. The Transition Years at St Brendan's and St Brigid's, for example, give us a great hand out during the school year – and some of them, invariably, do keep it up.

"I've always been involved with sports, so that's one of the attractions. But the parents, volunteers, and athletes are a unique bunch of people. With 12 athletes in three sports going to the Ireland Games this week, I must say they love competing, and they absolutely love training. What you see is what you get from them; we're like one big family."

It's a statement that transfers easily to every part of Kerry. Skellig Stars has no athletes on Team Munster in 2018, but Marian Kelly's pride in her club's 24 volunteers and 22 athletes is clear.

North Kerry Eagles will send four athletes and two gymnasts to the Games, and the facilities the club uses in Tarbert and Listowel Presentation Primary regularly bring together more than 20 athletes and some 40 volunteers.

"Most of the parents would be involved," Fiona Keane tells us. "My own daughter, Rebekah, is involved, and she's all excited right now, even though she hurt her finger and is worried she can't throw the javelin!"

Whether Rebekah and her team-mates win medals or not will only become clear in the coming days. The bravery in their attempts is already undoubted – as was the case when those South African footballers outplayed Scoil Naomh Eoin Baiste 15 summers ago.

The Kerryman, June 13, 2018.

When Lios Póil had West Kerry in the palm of its hand

My neighbour, Cinn Áird resident Eugene Devane, is by far Lios Póil's most successful manager. My dad suggested this one to me shortly after Eugene turned 80, and why wouldn't I go for it?

The club had never won a West Kerry Championship before he took over, but they claimed eight of the first 10 they played with him as manager. That could be a coincidence – but I think we'd all find that unlikely!

"THAT bloody pitch is playable", Lios Póil's Liam Higgins said 42 years ago at the club's new sports-field, on what was meant to be West Kerry final day.

It was November 1978, and matters were tense: Dingle wanted the game put back after a nasty night's rain and, if they had their way, Lios Póil's wait for a first West Kerry title would stretch by another few days or weeks at least.

But the townsmen lost the debate as referee Weeshie Fogarty ruled in Lios Póil's favour. Lios Póil won the match too, by four points, to complete a divisional treble. They'd win West Kerry again in '79.

This little club, which never won a divisional championship before '78, had eight by the end of 1987, the last dance of a dreamlike six-in-a-row. They won a County Junior Championship and played Division One football on-route. They even decided who'd captain Kerry to Sam in '85 and '86.

"A new spirit was evident in the team, and it was no coincidence that this spirit emerged the same year that Eugene Devane took over as team manager," Lios Póil chairperson John L O'Sullivan said at the 1979 AGM.

"We wouldn't have won one trophy, never mind three, without him," agreed captain Brendie O'Sullivan.

Eugene was just shy of 40 then. He's 80 now and, while never being especially open to praise, is happy to reflect on when Lios Póil ruled a peninsula.

Everyone 'round here is.

Some context

"I was asked by a couple of senior fellas in the club would I have a go at it," Eugene says. "Why they picked me, I don't know. I was a young man with a young family. But I said I would anyway.

"I was at the AGM at the old school in Lios Póil, and the biggest room was packed. Somebody else proposed Danny Garrett [Fitzgerald]. We were put out in the hall while the votes were being counted, and I think I won by two votes – or was it one vote? I don't know.

"I asked Danny would he go with me as selector or assistant, whatever, and I brought in Michael Griffin, too. It went from there, and '78 we started off."

Divisional dominance isn't rare, and it doesn't take much rooting through the records to notice that.

Laune Rangers won eight Mid Kerrys in a row in the '90s and five in the '00s; St Marys came within one win of its own six-in-a-row last winter; Crokes won eight on the spin in East Kerry from 2006 to 2013.

But Lios Póil's eight wins in 10 years were different. Its population has hovered around 750 for half a century, and it's penned in on all sides by footballing brawn.

Just west, Dingle: Corca Dhuibhne's capital and most decorated outfit. Out east, Annascaul: where All-Ireland medals could deck out the village Christmas tree. Further west, An Ghaeltacht: the club that most often betters Dingle. Over the hill, Castlegregory: whose pedigree, always there, was borne out in a 2010 All-Ireland Junior title.

"Even then, there were only about 20 players," Eugene says. "Lios Póil is one of the smallest parishes in the county, like. Denis Higgins was one man who'd go through flipping fire for you, but the whole lot of them put their flipping heart and soul into it. You had the Cathasaighs, the Higginses, the Sullivans, the whole lot of them came out of, what, five or six houses?

"And if you saw the training they used to do, I took no nonsense. Twenty rounds of the field we'd start with, and we'd have wire-to-wire, then, from the stand to the other side. If I blew the whistle and they halfway across, they'd have to turn and reverse. The training was something desperate. But fair play to them, everyone did it…You'd fellas up the country, they'd thumb down and wouldn't charge a bob. They just wanted to represent the club.

"I suppose the rest of the teams had to respect us in the end. The Lios Póil players, like, they were inside in the dressing rooms and they'd knock flipping walls down. They'd be like, 'Are we going to be beaten by these?' I can't repeat what some of them used to say, I suppose – but they'd nearly take the hinges off the doors on the way out."

Early triumphs

"Ah sure, I don't know how I would put it," Eugene says of the '78 breakthrough. "The whole of Lios Póil were kind of involved at the time in regards supporters, and when it was over, it was as good as seeing Kerry win in Croke Park. You couldn't get into Garraí [O'Sullivan's Bar] with the crowd that was there, and the celebrations went on for a week then."

The reportage from that time suggests the win didn't surprise Lios Póil but surprised everyone else.

At the '79 AGM, the late John L O'Sullivan, a genuine visionary, described the then-recent success as "inevitable". Fair to say *The Kerryman*, then, hadn't seen the inevitable coming.

The '78 semi-final against an improving An Ghaeltacht was a tight call, "but on current performance, the Gaeltacht men appear to have the edge," this newspaper wrote. Lios Póil won by four.

The Kerryman favoured Dingle for the final, too. Lios Póil won again by four.

The following year's final against Annascaul was tighter, with Roibeárd Ó Cathasaigh needed to kick a winner, but it was enough to prove this paper wrong again. We'd tipped Annascaul.

Lios Póil did lose the title in '80 and won no trophies at all in '81 – they even ended that year without a round of applause, if accounts of the '81 social are accurate – but Devane is convinced his team never stopped being West Kerry's best; not even then.

"In '80, we went up to Division One, and we were playing some massive teams. Take the Stacks in Tralee. They had Mikey Sheehy, Ger Power, the O'Keeffes, every game was like a championship game. We stayed there for two years before we were demoted again to two, and then, of course, we set off on the six-in-a-row.

"I think that's what affected us not winning West Kerry in '80 and '81. It's easy to talk in hindsight, but I reckon if we'd stayed in Division Two, we'd have won 10 in a row."

Not-so-secret ingredients

Before that '78 title, Lios Póil had no fixed abode and relied on two separate pieces of land belonging to John L and another club figurehead, Johnny Barrett. But at a cost of roughly £100,000, the club nested in Garraí na dTor, with a new pitch the centrepiece of a project also including a community hall and handball alley. While substantial funding came from Roinn na Gaeltachta, the GAA, and AnCO, the club sourced £15,000 from voluntary subs, £10,000 from fund-raisers, and another few thousand from exiles worldwide.

The facilities matched anything else in the county, and the sports-field received the official baptism it deserved in May '79 with a Kerry-Dublin and West Kerry-Crossmaglen double-bill.

"The field brought the players on a lot, and it gave the parish a mighty boost," Eugene says.

"John L and Johnny Barrett were the main drivers. Furthermore, West Kerry would never have won a County Championship only for John L, simply because he was on the phone all the time to the Kerry players to see would they play, and he wouldn't take no for an answer.

"Himself and Barrett were great men in the club. Plenty more backed them up, but they were the go-to guys."

It would have counted for less without players worthy of the fresh sod, but the field's first decade hosted one winning Lios Póil team upon another. The late Liam Higgins was the best known – being a two-time All-Ireland-winner – but the Ó Cathasaigh brothers, Gabriel, Gearóid, and Roibeárd, all lined out for Kerry at both senior and minor, with Gabriel winning an All-Ireland minor medal. Their brother, Seán, played minor too.

Denis Higgins played at all levels and won an All-Ireland Junior title – alongside Gabriel – under his brother Liam's management. Tomás Ó hAiniféin won a Junior All-Ireland of his own and also played under-21.

A few more were unlucky to never wear green and gold; others weren't of county standard but were vital to that decade of dreams made real.

Through most of it, Devane was only one part of a managerial three-piece as he called for assistance from a club stalwart, the late Michael Griffin, and an army man named Danny 'Garrett' Fitzgerald.

"Danny Garrett, brains? That man could do anything," Eugene says. "I could go away up and down the sideline, and I'd see a weak link, and I'd ask if we needed a substitution or a switch. Then Danny would say, look, we'll switch these two, and I'd go away thinking, 'Feck it, he's probably right'.

"He could probably read a game better than I could when I was in charge. He was a kind of genius, you could say. I would always adhere to him, and to Michael as well, of course."

Strength becomes dominance

Over six years – '82 to '87 – six leagues and six championships were for the taking out west. Lios Póil won 10 titles; Corca Dhuibhne's smallest club had the peninsula to itself, almost.

Respect's hard won when you ought to be little, but a thumping win over Castlegregory in '82 and another title against An Ghaeltacht meant they'd taken all four local rivals in finals. The team was beyond questioning.

"One could not but admire this side, who must now rank amongst the greatest West Kerry club teams," *The Kerryman* wrote in '83.

Then came deep frustration for Dingle, reduced to a Jimmy White role versus Lios Póil's Stephen Hendry. They were well beaten in '84 and came much closer in the next three deciders but were pushed down each time.

"My brother was managing Dingle for two years," Eugene says when asked what the highlight of the run was.

"Yerra, no, I didn't mind the first time beating him, but blood is thicker than water. I could feel it for him being beaten the second time.

"I don't know, it was a big day out by the Lios Póil fellas. They'd go for their few pints after, and the discussion about football inside in the pubs would bother you. I used to go downtown myself, but I'd go into the snug of the quietest pub in town; I didn't want to be talking about it at all.

"I didn't want any of that praise, fellas belting you on the back, 'fair play to you', this, that, and the other thing. I did my job, and I used to step back after that.

"We had tough, hard games with Dingle, and they had star players, you know, but they still couldn't beat us. You had Lios Póil fellas going to Mass here, and then they'd go back to Mass in Dingle again just to be in Dingle."

Sweet though western supremacy was, a county title eluded Lios Póil until '84, and it would've been cause for regret had it never arrived. They lost the Junior final to Valentia in '81 but, three years on, they completed the set by beating Ardfert in Tralee.

Lios Póil now had sway beyond Blennerville Bridge. Eugene became a county under-21 selector for one year and, more notably, was part of the management set-ups when West Kerry won County Championships in '84, '85, and '90. Lios Póil men – Gabriel Ó Cathasaigh and Denis Higgins – captained for the first two wins.

"Those were West Kerry's first times winning, only they weren't really," Eugene says. "Dingle, as they called themselves, won way back in the '40s, but they weren't Dingle; you had fellas from Lios Póil, Annascaul, the Gaeltacht playing with them. How could they be Dingle? I've had that out with Dingle people, and I don't give two monkeys what they say!

"But it was great anyway. One thing that stands out to me is from the year Denis Higgins was captain, there was this Nedeen Kelliher had a pony and trap outside the Brandon, and he'd give tourists a drive as far as Blennerville. He brought Denis and Bishop Moynihan [the cup] across Blennerville Bridge. That always stayed with me.

"Páidí Sé was Kerry captain in '85, and when he stood up on the Hogan Stand with the cup, he thanked Lios Póil for the captaincy. We had the final say, you see, as West Kerry champions. Tommy Doyle, then, got in in '86, thanks to us.

"I was selector with the Kerry under-21s – in '86, I suppose? Don't matter, I was only there the one year. It was a big thing that time, like going for the Dáil: you'd to go down around Waterville, Ballinskelligs, up around Tarbert looking for votes. I got in, but I didn't really want to go back. I was too busy, and there was too much travelling. If there was a challenge game, you'd have to down tools and go. It wouldn't work out.

"Winning with Lios Póil was ahead of anything, anyway. Lios Póil meant more to me than the county."

Back to reality – sort of

It's not that things went south quickly after '87, but Lios Póil gave in to what's natural. Players can't last forever, and they didn't.

Eugene remained in charge for some years afterwards and has returned, on and off, in various roles, most memorably as a selector when Lios Póil won their ninth and most recent West Kerry title in '04. They played another junior final that same year but fell marginally short of hot favourites Finuge.

It's probably unfair to compare Lios Póil's performances since '87 against the wonder years' standard; it could happen again, but it won't be soon – and why should it be, it being such a small parish and all?

Using a fair measure, the club still does well. It dropped to Division Five at the end of the '00s, but that kind of misery's been rare and not the norm. The club has won three junior Comórtas Peile na Gaeltachtas – Eugene was involved with all three teams – and later won the County and Munster Novice Championships, as well as a County Junior title, between 2016 and 2018.

Then emigration and retirements bit in. The foundations under small clubs are made of paper, and 2019 was a sour end to a bright decade.

"It's an awful pity, we're barely able to put out a team," Eugene says. "You'd have to give great credit to the lads keeping the show going. It would be an awful disaster if you've no football team, the fine facilities above there [in Garraí na dTor] could fall asunder.

"Emigration doesn't help, but what can you do? It's going on all over. You look at North Kerry, 'twas a stronghold of football one time. You had your Moyvanes, Ballylongfords, and Tarberts and them. Valentia can barely field a team, and they were very good one time.

"You're a small parish, and you haven't the numbers. You lost a couple of good players, the likes of Donncha Higgins, Noel Higgins, Eoghan Griffin, who went away. Brian Rayel, who won an All-Ireland Minor medal [in 2014]. They're a big loss to a small club."

To hear someone neither born nor reared in the parish caring so much for the club tells of a man long converted since he lined out with John Street (Dingle) at underage. As he words it, he got married, moved over to Lios Póil, "and the rest is history". He's 'black' Lios Póil and has been for long enough to absolve him of any past with other clubs. Eight West Kerrys in 10 years settled that.

"I don't know...was I lucky – or did I just have that gift?"

He's joking – but he had something.

It worked, too.

The Kerryman, June 17, 2020.

Lee aiming to hit new heights at Paralympics

The COVID-19 pandemic put a lot of little things on hold. It put some big things on hold, too, including the Paralympics. For Killarney athlete Jordan Lee, a top-class high-jumper, waiting an extra year to go for gold can't have been easy, but when I spoke to him ahead of the 2021 Games, his attitude was one of unrelenting positivity.

THERE'S an old clip on Facebook showing Jordan Lee in a past life. It's titled 'The only one-handed basketball player to play for Ireland', but after watching a few seconds, the disability alluded to, below the Killarney man's left elbow, vanishes.

Or that's the illusion, anyway. Lee the kid played underage basketball for Ireland, and he made it look effortless.

But it is the hardest-working sportspeople who end up being referred to as naturally gifted, and you would imagine Lee had to fight harder again to give that impression; he had to have been wired differently to play in a way that earned that kind of comment.

Then he switched from basketball to high jump and looked gifted in a new field; that all but confirmed that he is made of tough stuff.

"Deep down, there's a bit of me that's never satisfied, and it's something I'll never get out of me," Lee acknowledges.

"If I didn't have that, I wouldn't have represented my country and achieved what I achieved at basketball. I think every athlete needs to have that, especially when you're at elite level. The bar always needs to be raised."

Without that mentality, he wouldn't be as near to the top as he is now. He's one of the best high jumpers in Ireland by any measure – his supremacy at T47, a category for below-the-elbow amputees, is only part of the equation – and he's of Paralympic standard internationally. That's where he stands now, just four years on from his first jump.

He spoke to *The Kerryman* in May 2019 after setting a national T47 record by jumping one metre and 88 centimetres. During an interview with Jimmy Darcy in this newspaper in January 2020, just eight months later, he told us his personal best was 1.95 metres. On both occasions, he said the 2020 World Games in Tokyo was on his checklist.

He was strong-willed then and still is, but you can improve anything if you work on it, and that goes for mentality as well. Indeed, lock-down, the thing that postponed the 2020 Paralympic Games and his dream by a year, came with an unlikely opportunity attached.

"It was a huge shock to the system. I mean, we all knew, deep down, it was on the way, but it's still a shock to hear the words," he says.

"I remember sitting in my room, just after coming off the Zoom call that Paralympics Ireland organised to inform us that the games weren't going ahead. I'd scheduled a session for after the call, and I remember looking out the window at the rain pouring down, thinking to myself that I might just skip the session. It would have been easier to relax and watch a bit of Netflix, but the one day I'm not training gives my opponents an extra day to better me. That's the mentality I've always tried to use.

"But now I think the extra year was fantastic, especially for someone like me, who's only 20. I've matured as an athlete and as a person. The mental factor in high jump is that you're trying to jump something that's five, six inches over your own head, and thinking about jumping that can be quite daunting. If you knock the bar, it's put down as a failure. Every time you leave a competition, no matter how high you jump, the last jump's a failure. It's about walking away from that competition and re-setting yourself and trying to be positive.

"Every athlete has to be critical of what they do, but something over the past year that I've been doing is trying to become more positive, even if I wasn't exceptionally happy with a performance. I think COVID has something to do with that. We're in a tricky time and situation, and we're all trying to think of what we have, not what we don't have."

And that kind of mentality was a neat fit as the country locked down for the first time last spring. It was a time when his status as an elite athlete meant next to nothing as restrictions were as stringent for him as anyone else. Killarney Valley Athletics Club – where he trains – may as well have been in Senegal.

It could have been a time of forgivable regression. The Fosbury Flop – the game-changing and now-dominant high-jump technique Dick Fosbury pioneered in the 1960s – wasn't something Lee could replicate in his garden, and in a sport with as many moving parts to consider as high jump, the side-lining of repetition might or should have been devastating.

Lee's personal best is still 1.95m, and that could lead you to assume he stood still in that time, if assumptions are your thing.

But listening in as he talks of those months does shade things in a different complexion. He's sure he has developed, and just because that development hasn't yet given him a new PB doesn't mean it won't soon.

"I was fortunate enough to have access to my own gym equipment, and I saw it as an opportunity to better myself in other areas as opposed to being down and negative about what I couldn't do," he says.

"I tried to improve my overall strength. I focussed more on my recovery work to ensure my body could go through those harder sessions and allow me to get that bit stronger. My sessions in lock-down were very different to what they typically would have been, but I still benefited.

71

"In my first session back at the track, I was able to jump pretty well, and that was down to working on aspects I may not have worked on before, even doing simple things like curve runs, run-throughs, setting up my approach in the back garden and running it as I would. That stood to me when I returned to the track in the summer.

"This lock-down is much different. I can access the track. My coach, Tomás [Griffin], has converted his shed into a top-quality gym, and I have access to that as a government-funded professional athlete. I can travel beyond the five kilometres to train now.

"At the moment, I currently feel like I'm physically in the best shape I've ever been in. I've put on two kilos of muscle over the past four months, and I've increased my overall strength by a massive amount. But the stronger and faster you become, the stride length in your run, and the technical aspects, they have to change. That's something I've to work on in the coming months.

"Once I nail my approach, keep focussing on every aspect of my run-up, repeating, staying in the curve, and being diligent to my run-up and my stride length and the pace coming into the bar, I feel like I'll be on for a big personal best, to be honest. There's a still [photograph] of me at a recent invitational event jumping 1.92, and I'm about 10 centimetres over the bar…I'm feeling explosive. There's a lot going on in high jump, it can be a head-wreck, but when you hit a perfect jump, there's no better feeling in the world."

It is this kind of talk that supports Lee's claim that his mind-set changed for the better in COVID times.

He gave the impression of being down on himself after finishing sixth in the 2019 World Para Athletics Championships in Dubai; it's all there in writing. He was ranked second in the world shortly before the competition, and sixth just wasn't where he wanted to be. Never mind that he was a 19-year-old who finished sixth in the world while carrying an injury and that he jumped one metre and 87 centimetres under the most severe pressure, mere days on from struggling to clear 1.75m. There were positives if he'd looked through the disappointment – but he can see those bright spots now, like the rest of us might have.

SO NOW to look at where Lee is now, with the Paralympics due to begin – we hope – in a touch over five months' time.

For all its complications, the past year saw him finish second in the national able-bodied under-23 championship, so there is an Irish medal to show for the year's struggle. More recently, he was one of two male high-jumpers invited to an elite national meeting, and he was also one of just two Paralympic athletes asked to compete at the same event. It underlines the respect there is for Lee at the highest level in this country. He trains six days a week to remain in that elite bracket, but he pushes it further than even that suggests.

Some days include double sessions, and there's extensive recovery work, which can take up to an hour and a half. It sounds like a lot, but it's in line with what he's asking of himself for 2021. He believes this can be the biggest year of his career to date.

"The standard in my category, T47, for below-the-elbow amputees, there are about three two-metre jumpers in the rankings," he says. "So the quality is unbelievable. They're as good as, if not better than, the top able-bodied guys. But it's good to have that competition, too, because it really brings up that Paralympic athletes are really good athletes in their own right; they're great athletes who just happen to have a disability.

"But I'm aiming high, and I think that's a realistic goal, if I'm being honest. My personal best is 1.95 but, as I said, I think I could jump two in the next couple of months. My goal for Tokyo and the Paralympics is to contend for a medal. That's what I'm looking for.

"For the European Championships in June, the aim is to win, to be honest. I would be going in as one of the top guys in the competition, so I'm going for gold. They are my aims – and I want to break the 1.97m European record as well."

They're big words, and only those closest to his training can tell you for sure if they're more than that, but you at least sense that they're built on something solid. Lee is confident but not overpoweringly so; we know he has achieved the impressive already, but when you listen to him demanding even more from the future, you tend to believe he can get there – fresh personal bests or not.

Perhaps it's because he seems a genuine type; you can't get to know a fella in one conversation, but he hits the right notes. For every big demand he makes of himself, there's a mention of Tomás Griffin; Killarney Valley Athletics Club; his mother; his father; his step-father; his siblings; his sponsors; or just about anyone who helps him in any capacity. He speaks highly as well of his training partner, Sam Griffin, whom he describes as "a great, up-and-coming long jumper".

Away from the track, he's an ambassador for CARA, an organisation looking to boost the number of sporting and physical-activity options available for people with disabilities. He provides motivational talks, too. Despite the demands of being an elite athlete, he's studying Health and Leisure part-time at Munster Technological University. He's also proud that he moved into his own apartment over the past year.

Just as it is easy to forget that he lives with a disability, it is easy to lose track of the fact that he's only 20, but he seems at ease with a life more packed than his age should have it.

"It's fantastic," he says. "I love to stay busy. I can find it quite hard to be at home all day. If we weren't in the situation we're all in currently, I'd never be home.

"Then when I'm at home, I'm trying to improve as a person. It's about making tiny bits of progress and being happy about things that went well. But, at the same time, I'm always looking for areas that I can build on."

Amniotic band syndrome meant that Lee would live with one arm; his umbilical cord wrapped around the limb and stopped his left arm from developing as it should have.

It might have been defining. Instead, he has made it the least notable thing about him.

The Kerryman, March 17, 2021.

Part Two

Culture and History

Caid, craic, and the odd pint at Comórtas Peile na Gaeltachta.

The next two features document Comórtas Peile na Gaeltachta, effectively the All-Ireland Football Championship for clubs based in Irish-speaking communities. Both pieces could just as easily have fitted into the 'Sports' section, so I felt they'd be the perfect start to the transition into 'Culture and History'.

I started working on the first of these two features ahead of the 2016 Comórtas in Múscraí; indeed, it was the first piece I started working on during my first day in The Kerryman. I'd always felt the Comórtas never got the kind of coverage it deserved, so this article was a statement of why it needs our attention.

BARELY a half-skip from the Kerry border, you'll find an enclave called Múscraí.

This west Cork Gaeltacht, flanked by the Derrynasaggart and Boggeragh mountains, has been called home by Ó Riada and Ó Ríordán; Saints Gobnait and Finbarr; and the legendary Cór Cúil Aodha, despite being every bit as secluded as the stereotypical Gaeltacht region. The local language, a lilting strain of Munster Irish, under-scores this Gaeltacht still further, and the love for football around these parts is as intense as a Peadar Ó Riada verse.

All this considered, Múscraí's capital, Baile Bhúirne, is an ideal home for Comórtas Peile na Gaeltachta.

The 'Comórtas' is the All-Ireland Championship for football teams from the Gaeltachtaí, and it's a festival of Gaeilge – but it's more than that. Though it remains best known for promoting the native language, another valuable, fading part of Irish life has always thrived at the event: the teams at the Comórtas enjoy themselves – and when last has anyone associated football with having fun?

That's not to say the competition is merely a giddy get-together; you needn't call for binoculars to find quality football. Dara Ó Cinnéide of Kerry and An Ghaeltacht fame reminds *The Kerryman* of the team that Gaoth Dobhair sent to Waterford's Gaeltacht na Rinne in 2013, a panel that included players called upon by Jim McGuinness during Donegal's recent resurgence.

"I remember asking the McGees what Jim would make of them playing, and they told me, straight out, that they didn't care," Ó Cinnéide says. "That Gaoth Dobhair team was serious; they wanted to win the Comórtas.

"It's a shame that county stars aren't normally allowed to take part, because a lot of them would go all out to win it. I always valued the Comórtas, and I wasn't alone in that."

But while football's march towards professionalism in all but name is as ominous as the flight of a Colm Cooper kick-pass, the Comórtas is one of the few competitions enjoyed as much by players as it is by supporters. Ó Cinnéide isn't insulted at being reminded that many of the participants who have travelled to Cork have done so with more than one eye on having the craic.

"You're right, and that's important! I always had a few pints at the Comórtas, as did more of the Kerry lads who'd travelled," he explains. "It's as much about the craic as it is about football, and why would there be anything wrong with that?"

One incident from the 2006 edition in An Spidéal was particularly dismaying to the inter-county star.

"We were just after beating Naomh Abán in the semi-final, and I was sitting down with the lads, having a bite to eat. Naomh Abán had a County semi-final coming up in Cork the week after, and when I looked out the window, I saw them training down by the beach. I couldn't believe they weren't being allowed to enjoy themselves. I just turned to one of the boys and said, 'Heigh, tá an Comórtas f***ed'.

"That said, even though it was tremendous fun first and foremost, the Comórtas did have a positive impact on my football and my club-mates' football. I remember when we were winning this thing in the '90s, just before An Ghaeltacht broke through as a serious force in Kerry and everywhere else. It was a huge boost to win a competition and put down a mark, but those weekends were also team-bonding sessions. It brought us all together, and we improved from there.

"An Ghaeltacht have a strong team coming through again, and a good performance here could bring them on, definitely."

This year's Comórtas has drawn huge attendances, and judging by a minute's shameless eavesdropping around An Ollphoball – a marquee equipped with bars, televisions, and shops – everyone is at least making an effort to speak the language. Youths from neo-Gaeltachtaí in Dublin and Belfast are conversing entirely through Irish.

Tomás Ó hAiniféin grew up in Lios Póil, the most easterly village in Kerry's Corca Dhuibhne Gaeltacht, and he feels the language of his parish's soul has benefited from its participation in the Comórtas.

"For breac-Gaeltachtaí like Lios Póil, it can be a challenge to keep Irish alive, but I think the Comórtas has made that job much easier for us," he says. "Players and supporters come here, they use the language, and I've no doubt Lios Póil's Irish has improved considerably as a result."

Though the Comórtas' demise is always feared to be imminent, Ó hAiniféin is one of many hoping it can hold tough against considerable challenges: "I hope it'll survive well beyond the end of my years. To lose the Comórtas would be a tragedy."

The Kerryman, June 8, 2016.
The Corkman, June 9, 2016.

Oh, for the love of caid!

I was back reporting from the Comórtas the following year, but this time I made a much longer trip to Tuar Mhic Éadaigh, County Mayo. I spent much of the weekend in the company of my good friend Cathal Larkin, a long-suffering Mayo supporter, and I thank him for pointing out what I might otherwise have missed.

Saturday afternoon and Sunday afternoon:

WE'RE in Ballintubber, Mayo, but only the absence of a Béal Bán sea gale distinguishes this Saturday afternoon from the typical west Kerry football experience.

It's Comórtas Peile na Gaeltachta 2017, and Lios Póil's footballers are benefiting from the bias of a stand housing the same faces, voices, and wisecracks you encounter every weekend in Gallaras or Páirc Seán Baróid.

With his own club scheduled to play Belmullet on the same field later on, An Ghaeltacht supporter Gearóid Ó Cinnéide has called in early to encourage his neighbours' parish for their Junior Championship quarter-final.

The Kerry lads have much to spare over their Belfast opponents, and complacency is gnawing at what had been a perfect performance. With his team five points to the good, Adrian Ó Raoil jabs at a '45' but doesn't find the O'Neill's sweet spot, forcing the ball to hook from goal like a shopping bag caught in a gale.

"Go bhfóire Dia sna flaithis" – May God in the Heavens help us – Ó Cinnéide roars with the subtlety of a drill, and his expletives force giggles from all within earshot. Unduly worried that he might have upset the stand's Lios Póil contingent, he turns to supporter Donncha 'Bán' Ó Súilleabháin and reassures him with a genuine "Ach tá sibh ag imirt go maith. Oh tá go deimhin, ambaiste."

Unoffended at Ó Cinnéide's outburst, Lios Póil's players persist and build a lead sufficiently comfortable to allow for the kind of spraoi that's as much a part of the Comórtas as the football itself.

With fewer than five minutes remaining, the club's 59-year-old selector, Gabriel Ó Cathasaigh, changes into a green and yellow jersey and calls full-forward Deaglán Ó Súilleabháin in for a tea break. Wearing an ordinary pair of shoes, Ó Cathasaigh jogs into a playing role for the first time in years; the laughs in the stand grow louder with his every step from side-line to forward line.

His contribution in those closing minutes won't feature in discussions of his best performances in Lios Póil's stripes, but he insists afterwards there was logic behind the unexpected switch.

"It wasn't planned at all, to be honest, but I think it was necessary," he says. "We're very low on substitutes, and I wanted to spare fellas, seeing as we might have to play three matches in three days. I didn't have boots, but I had a solid pair of shoes, so I went for it. It was an unusual move, but I think it was the right one."

Ó Cathasaigh's point about Lios Póil's lack of numbers is proven precise within hours. The Kerry team falls to Donegal's Naomh Náille on Sunday afternoon, and the Ulster outfit's sizeable panel proves key once the Junior semi-final moves into extra time. Determined to hide his disappointment, however, Ó Cathasaigh reminds that football "has never been the Comórtas' sole concern".

"You never enjoy losing, but we gave it our best against a very strong team," he says. "I'm proud of the effort, and I was equally proud to hear the lads encouraging and instructing each other in Irish. We're one of only a few bilingual clubs in the country, and you can sometimes forget how special that makes us.

"This is an important competition for many reasons, and not all of them are to do with football. There were thousands above in the main field in Tuar Mhic Éadaigh [Toormakeady] using Irish with people from different parts of the country. It boosts the language, and it's an important outlet for Gaeltacht regions. Corca Dhuibhne will host it in two years' time after a long break, and that will provide the West Kerry clubs with a chance to hold a massive competition that will bring people from all over to our part of the world."

Sunday evening and Monday afternoon:

A KERRY team hasn't won the Senior competition's *Corn an Aire* trophy since 1999, a fact that rankles with everyone in Cumann Caide na Gaeltachta.

The club's semi-final wrestle with Waterford's Rinn Ó gCuanach is developing beneath a hail of Padraig Ó Sé commentary; the Dún Chaoin man stands at the side door of his radio road-caster, surveying the action like an owl that's heard a mouse rustling through a nearby bush.

His Irish is soothing enough to bring about world peace, but he's probably just as happy using it to announce An Ghaeltacht as one-point winners of a pulsating match. A half-day later, the westernmost club in Ireland dismantles Cork's Cill na Marta in a one-sided bank holiday Monday final, confirming this as a perfect long weekend for Ó Sé and company.

"It's not the first time I've commentated on An Ghaeltacht winning a competition, but this is special," he says. "We hadn't won it with 18 years, and it was time to put that right. It is a medal none of these lads had. Not even Marc Ó Sé had won a Comórtas.

"I remember going to the Comórtas when it was on in Gallaras for the first time back in 1985, so I've been involved for many years in one way or another. It was special to commentate on my own club winning a competition I've grown up with, and it was made even more special by the fact that my two sons, Tomás and Óigí [Padraig Óg], were playing."

But, with football hurtling towards a future in which it's professional in all but name, are competitions such as the Comórtas doomed to drift into irrelevance over the coming decades?

"Yerra, of course not," Ó Sé exclaims. "I've made friends from all over the country through this thing, we all have, friends you mightn't meet from one end of the year to the other. The social side is just as important as the sporting side.

"This isn't just about football; far from it. It's about culture, language, friendships, and craic. Everyone involved loves the Comórtas Peile, and that will ensure its survival.

"I can't wait to welcome friends from all over the country to Gallaras when the Comórtas returns home in 2019 in good health. And, please God, this young An Ghaeltacht team will be going for the three-in-a-row!"

The Kerryman, June 7, 2017.

'Back then, a camera was a mighty novelty.'

My Deputy Editor, Dónal Nolan, put me on to this story. I drove out from Tralee to Castlegregory one afternoon to meet Maurice O'Keeffe at the Spar shop in the village, and then I followed him out to Tom Daly's house.

I did this because I knew Tom had an old film reel of quite some historical value, although his own recollections of times past were every bit as interesting as what that reel contained.

TOM Daly pushes a wooden door, opening the porch of his pale-yellow house to Tralee historian Maurice O'Keefe and this *Kerryman* reporter. Backing off a cement doorstep, he looks to his right and smiles at his two guests before pointing his black walking stick at the century-old building's entrance.

"Go in there now from that breeze," he says, his command barely audible through the shrieking Scairbhín gale pulsing in from Lough Gill.

Maurice takes to the porch's shelter before leading the way, through a short hallway, to a wooden table in the front room – a place where he recently mined precious nuggets for his Dingle-to-Tralee railway oral history compilation. While Tom lifts a Siúcra bag and a carton of SAXA from the table to make room for our notepads and recorders, Maurice recounts Tom's contribution to his newest project.

"After securing sponsorship from Kerry County Council earlier this year, I started compiling accounts about the old Dingle-to-Tralee railway," he says. "Since January, I've interviewed 11 people, Tom being one of them. He's the only person who can remember travelling on the branch that ran to Castlegregory until 1939, so he's unique in that regard alone. But during our conversation, he told me he also had a precious piece of history to his name.

"And that's what brings us here today. Tom's uncle, George Daly, left for New York in the 1920s, but on a rare return visit to his native Castlegregory in 1949, he recorded local activities with an eight-millimetre cine camera, producing a reel that is of infinite historical value.

"That fantastic reel survives, and Tom kindly allowed us to create a remastered version, which we will share with the public for the first time in Castlegregory Community Hall on Sunday."

Tom sits across from us with his joined hands resting on the table's edge. He nods continuously, seemingly in sync with the ticks of a red clock hanging above the kitchen door, and as Maurice winds his introduction to a close, Tom swivels to his left and points his finger at the garden outside his kitchen window.

"George was out there filming in the back garden, and my family had fierce wonder. Back then, a camera would have been a mighty novelty, sure," he says.

"He did a heap of filming of people coming out of the Church and congregating above at the village for an old chat; footage of us drawing water from the pump; the old Ford cars; the thatched houses that were in the village; and the old farming methods.

"George gave us the tape in his will, and we put it on here for a few family members and a local teacher called Pat O'Shea. That was only around 20 years ago, and it was our first time seeing it. I thought it was mighty going to see myself as a young ladeen chasing a pony around a field!"

Rummaging through the notes scattered around the table, Maurice wrenches two stapled pages from the muddle.

"It's all explained here," he says while waving a press release. "Tom and I went down to the centre to watch it, just the two of us, and I recorded Tom's commentary. We took the reel away then and, with assistance from Dan Devane in Tralee, we digitised it. We slowed it down because it was quite jumpy, and we combined it with Tom's commentary, and then we transferred it to DVD.

"The final cut is an action-packed 25-minute colour document of life in Castlegregory in the late 1940s, and

I can't wait to share it with the public. A lot of people in the film still have relations living locally, and I'm sure they'll love the film."

The occasion will also serve as a launch for the Irish Life and Lore Tralee and Dingle Narrow Gauge Railway Oral History Collection. Tom was one of 11 who contributed to that project and, chuckling at the mention of the old train, he's only delighted to share his memories today as well.

"Yerra, I must have been six or seven my first time on it," he says.

"After the fair day, we'd bring the cattle up to the old stop in the village, and the train would bring the livestock off towards Tralee. We had relations living in Ashe Street, and we used the train to call to them regular, too.

"It seemed mighty fast to me when I was first on it, and I was all excited to see the smoke rising near the front! When we got to Tralee, I had fierce fascination looking up at all the people and all the big buildings. We'd get the bit of shopping, pay the few bills, and what have you. It was mostly business only for a cup of tea on The Mall, but it was exciting."

The Castlegregory branch stopped in 1939, but the steam engine still rattles around Tom's mind today. The train opened the Dingle Peninsula to a new world, and that's not easily forgotten.

"The Dingle-to-Tralee service continued for a good few years after the Castlegregory line stopped," Tom says, "and you'd often see the cloud of steam rising off the train when you'd look up towards Camp.

"The line closed altogether in 1953, but even though CIE brought us in from then on, we did miss the train. Before it came along, there was no easy way of getting around the place. It changed our lives."

The Kerryman, May 10, 2017.

A centenarian's story

In spite of his advanced age, it came as something of a surprise to me that John Coffey (100) passed away just a few months after I interviewed him one Friday morning. He was as sharp as a tack and seemed to be in rude health for a man of 100.

It was one of the strangest and most enjoyable interviews I ever carried out. Strange because I was talking to a man who brought me as close as I'll ever get to a first-hand account of the Great Famine; enjoyable because he was such a nice man to talk to.

LONGEVITY runs in the Coffey family. Lewis Road's John Coffey, Beaufort by birth, turned 100 last month and emulated his great-grandmother in doing so.

John was 12 when she died, old enough to remember her telling him of the Famine. His passing on of her stories makes for surreal listening; it's not a first-hand verbal account of the starvation that ravaged this country, but it's as close as one can get nowadays.

"Oh my God, listen here," he says while stretching back on his sitting-room armchair, peering up at the Our

Lady statuette overlooking his mantle piece. "She said it was unnatural. You'd see a family there one evening, and there might be two of them dead when you'd get up in the morning – died of starvation.

"It was taken for granted someone'd die during the night – 'cause they had nothing to eat. When the potatoes failed, they had plenty of corn, but Britain took away the corn over to England…Almighty God, leave me alone with the stories she had."

John hit the three-figure mark on August 26, a date that has filled his life with memories joyful and sad. He married on an August 26, and it was also on that date that he lost his 13-year-old son, John Joe.

John's mother was also born on an August 26, and like her son, she lived a long life; she died at 94.

Such pedigree aside, the way John went about his work as west Kerry's rent collector helped him on his way to 100. It also set in motion a love of cycling that endures.

"After leaving school, I went working as a draper's assistant in County Laois from the age of 15," he explains.

"When I was there, the War broke out in 1939. My father was collecting the Dingle district [rent] as well as doing all around Killarney. He was getting old, though, and my brother, Batty, was helping him collect in Dingle.

"But Batty joined the army in 1939; De Valera was asking for volunteers during the Emergency. When Batty left, my father wrote to me to come back home, and I started collecting the Dingle district in 1939. I had to do that every month of the year, once a month.

"Nine years I kept cycling from my own house in Beaufort, back west of Dingle, and back to Dingle then to collect from the cottages in the town.

"I had to cross Conor Hill at night to get down to Brandon. Then I'd collect the northern side of the peninsula, staying in O'Shea's, Brandon, where I met Kitty, my wife.

"From my house to Dingle was roughly 40 miles, but by the time I got to Dingle, I had 60 done because you'd have to go up one by-road, down another.

"I'm sure the exercise I did back then is standing to me today. I can still cut a hedge, I can cut a lawn. I used to cycle down to Muckross House up to two years ago, but with the traffic on the road, I stopped, and I do 20 minutes on an exercise bike every morning instead.

"Go 'way with your Ring of Kerry – that's peanuts to me!"

On the way to 100, he's collected more memories than rents. To place his age in context, he attended Mayo's first All-Ireland win in 1936, never mind their most recent in 1951. He recalls being "really scared" of the Free State soldiers passing his house during the War of Independence as his uncle, Mike, would've been shot if captured, "for supporting the opposition".

John was fifth in a family of 12, all born within a mere 16 years. He'd walk to Cullina National School barefoot, weather permitting, and he's not shy of a dig at today's youngsters and their commutes: "To think they have a blooming bus collecting them!"

His father was a County Council man, and the family had a shop in Beaufort, so they weren't the worst off in the parish – but that's not to say life was carefree.

"We saw hard times," he says. "Everyone was in the same boat.

"The [Second World] War broke out, and the rationing was something fierce. You got half an ounce of tea for the week. Could you imagine? A spoonful, you could say.

"We had a car, but it was grounded because we had no petrol. The only ones who got coupons for petrol were doctors. I don't think Priests got them because they had ponies and traps. The rationing on the petrol kept going for a couple of years after [the War].

"The changes I have seen are unreal. The biggest change I can think of was rural electrification. It took a lot of the misery out of the country people, the farming community…They were grand in the town, they had power, but in the country, if you wanted to wash the children, you had to boil a pot of water. Now they have washing machines, fridges, you name it!

"Your age now, ye wouldn't believe it…when I was working in west Kerry, I started collecting around eight in the morning in Castlemaine. It was dust road from Castlemaine as far as Annascaul.

"The road from Tralee to Dingle was tarred, but from Dingle to Ballyferriter, dust road. Connor Hill, dust road. Down to Brandon, over as far as Castlegregory, all dust roads."

Nearly the only topic that needs addressing following an hour's conversation is his footballing loyalties.

Since the 1950s, John has lived a few steps from Fitzgerald Stadium and Dr Crokes' home ground on Lewis Road – but for all their appeal and all their trophies, the Crokes have never won John's outright allegiance.

"I'm the last of the Beaufort team of 1944 [that won the County Junior Championship], all dead only myself," he says. "I'm living here a long time; one of the conditions of getting the Community Welfare job in Killarney from 1947, until I retired in the 1980s, was that I'd move into the town.

"But if it came down to it and Beaufort were playing the Crokes – I'd still have to shout for Beaufort."

The Kerryman, September 18, 2019.

Preserving a haunting past

During my time with The Kerryman, I've learned a lot about things that, frankly, I knew nothing about. And, very often, these happen to be things that everyone in the county should know a lot about.

The Tarbert Bridewell and its past are among those things.

AT one point loathed, the Tarbert Bridewell's limestone walls are today admired as an elegant showcase of 19th-Century craftsmanship.

Formerly a setting for confinement of prisoners and issuing of harsh punishments, the imposing structure is now home instead to much of what marks a north Kerry community as special.

From 1831, the Bridewell served as a jail for more than 40 years – and when that stretch of its life was consigned to grim history, the building continued to function as a courthouse for a further 75 years.

The site now operates under a community-based board of trustees for the people of Tarbert, and a voluntary management committee oversees its day-to-day running. Some 30 years have now passed since the locality voted to save an historic building being sold for its neat stone – and it's 25 years since the Bridewell escaped from dereliction.

"Under the umbrella of Tarbert Development Association [TDA], the community in 1988 decided and voted to save the building, and our brief was the restoration and preservation of the building because of its historical, cultural and architectural value – and, believe it or not, nearly all of us that were there in 1988 are still there," Mary O'Connell says. "We were chaired back then by the late Maurice Fitzgerald, and his son, Niall, is now chair.

"We wanted to turn it into an amenity that would be self-sustaining, where any profits could be reinvested in the community. It's owned by the community, it's managed by the community – and the trustees are within the community."

Though just one of eight of Bridewells built in Kerry, Tarbert's was the only one restored as a museum, Mary explains.

It and its fellow Bridewells held their prisoners in miserable conditions. With cases heard every 30 days, to be arrested the day after a court sitting was considered especially unfortunate; it meant having to suffer a month of bread, gruel, and mindless labour before meeting justice.

"At the time, there were local notables appointed by the Government because of their wealth or status or political reliability, and the surnames of the leading magistrates in Tarbert were Sandes, Leslie, Chute, Blennerhassett, Spring, Crosby – names that are still there today between Tralee and Tarbert," Mary says.

"What we do here today is tell the story of Thomas Dillon, and you follow him through his arrest, his charge, and when he was brought to the Bridewell. He would have been kept in Tarbert until the court of petty sessions was held. He had left his cow onto a neighbour's property to graze and was then fined 10 shillings.

"Mary McCarthy is very interesting, too, in that she was there with her baby. When she was tried for such a small crime [stealing cabbage plants], she got deportation. Her baby went with her, and her children were then put into a workhouse.

"The thing about deportation at that time was that the judiciary was sending off young women, young men, and they would have been transported at times for very minor crimes.

"If a young man stole a book, they'd get deportation. If an older person did it, they wouldn't, because they'd hardly last the voyage. The regime in the Bridewell prison itself was very bad; they just got gruel, bread, milk – and that was it."

After suffering decades of disuse following its original closure, it took five years from the ambitious local moves of 1988 for the Bridewell to be in a fit state to welcome visitors. North Kerry folk at home and overseas were most supportive of fund-raising efforts.

Today, aside from functioning as a reminder of an infinitely grimmer time, the Bridewell houses an exhibition on the works of Thomas McGreevy; a coffee shop; a gift centre; and a community hub that hosts an impressive range of events and groups.

Its history has even drawn attention from ghost-hunter teams from around Ireland, and the building also appeared recently in the US version of "Who Do You Think You Are?" as actor Sean Hayes traced his lineage back to the trial of his great-granduncles – Patrick and William – for the assault of his great-great-grandfather.

"But you do get to a stage where refurbishment has to start again, and that's what we're about at the moment," Mary said on the 25th anniversary of the re-opening.

"With the support of KLAG, we've had funding approved under the LEADER programme for refurbishments and an up-to-date AV system to enhance the experience for visitors. These will be in place ahead of the new tourist season – but a quarter of the cost must be borne by the sponsor, so we'll be undertaking a fund-raising drive in due course."

And these planned efforts will be worthwhile, Mary maintains.

"From the day we opened, we've had the most wonderful staff on CE schemes, taking a personal interest; they love that it's our history, it's our past," she says.

"We can't forget; I know it's a haunting past from a different time, and it was a terrible time – but we preserve it for our children and our grandchildren."

The Kerryman, March 14, 2018.

Refreshed Wexford hurler sets eyes on magical Blasket return.

I've often found well-known GAA figures hard to interview. I feel nervous while talking to them, and some of them, frankly, don't make that easier because they have an opinion of themselves.

Diarmuid Lyng, as far as I can tell, isn't like that at all.

Meeting him was a strange experience in some ways. I wanted to get a photo, and he told me, "I'll walk around the beach with my hurley and sliotar, doing my own thing, and you can take pictures of it." I can't pretend that didn't make for an awkward few minutes – but Diarmuid's his own man, and that's what I liked about him.

SITTING in a car by Kilmurry Bay, facing the jagged remains of Minard Castle and a strand dipping its sandy toes in the Atlantic, the prospect of being left to wait by an interviewee is made unusually attractive.

Typical, then, that punctuality is set for a rare victory on west Kerry ground. With the car window lowered for the sea's purrs to whistle in, the hum of an approaching engine disturbs the ambience. A red hatchback Corolla fizzes into view on the bóthrín behind the beach and arcs into a parking space like a hare sidestepping a fox.

"Cén caoi an bhfuil tú boy?" a bearded driver shouts from the red car. It's 6.45pm, and Diarmuid "Gizzy" Lyng is bang on time.

He leaps out and stretches his slender frame, pointing his hurley to the clouds as if to salute the surroundings. Wearing a green Aran jumper, jogging pants, and a pair of sandals, he saunters over and plonks himself on this writer's passenger seat, leaving the door open for the midges to join us.

Any intrusion on Lios Póil's natural assets is unintentional on the part of the former Wexford hurler. It's common knowledge that he loves west Kerry and, after the briefest swirl of small talk, he rolls the conversation towards Ireland's westernmost peninsula, his home over these last two years.

"I've experienced a lot in west Kerry," he says as he bats the midges away. "I do some work with *TG4* and Raidió na Gaeltachta now, but it wasn't until I came to Feothanach in 2005 that I connected with the Irish language. I was in the second year of my teaching course in Froebel at the time and, before we went to Corca Dhuibhne for our Irish-language training, I was told I'd fail if my Irish didn't improve.

"Myself and a few others got together and said 'right, let's do this properly'. While we were there, we did normal stuff. We mixed with the locals, went to Ventry beach, the usual craic. But within three days, I had my first dream in Irish. Something had awoken – and I just stuck with it."

Only two years prior to that influential fortnight in Feothanach, Lyng left for America and a J1 summer at a point in his life when his appreciation for Irish culture and language was as frail as porcelain.

Thinking back to that summer, a few seconds of embarrassment stick out from his memory bank, and he today cites those seconds as his earliest steps in the direction of the life he has since embraced.

"I was working in a bar in Minneapolis, and a man with Donegal roots came in and spoke to me in Irish – and I couldn't answer him," he says. "Back then, I had this view that there was little of value in Ireland, that everything worthwhile was in Hollywood or Summer Bay – and my attitude to the Irish language was similarly cold.

"Thinking back, it's hard to believe now that I've spent two years living in west Kerry, let alone that I've worked on the Great Blasket and that I'm encouraging more people to go out there and connect with our heritage in the way that I did."

On Friday week, boats will depart from the peninsula for the Great Blasket and a four-day retreat titled

'Dúisigh do Dhúchas', a creative, spiritual, and practical experience of re-wilding and re-tuning through the medium of Irish.

Lyng – a regular visitor to the island that gifted us Ó Criomhthain, Sayers, and Ó Súilleabháin – co-organised the event with Siobhan de Paor and Cearbhuil Ni Fhionnghusa and, for him, the weekend represents a return to a part of west Kerry that moulded his perception of life.

"Before going out to the Blaskets in 2015, I was in a very low place personally. I was suffering – but I went out to work in the hostel for six weeks, and I found my cure.

"You don't have to follow a process on the Blaskets; it's an open space. While I was there, I connected with nature and our rich heritage. I was able to look out from Peig Sayers' window and see the Atlantic, An Trá Bán, the seal colonies – and I had the time to embrace it. There were no constraints.

"I watched the island come back to life over those six weeks. Visitors called over, the houses were full, and we had music and song each night while the candles flickered on the windowsills. Irish is a soul language and, to my mind, the Great Blasket is the kind of space that allows it to flourish.

"We'll reawaken our learning through workshops and exercises, nourishing an appreciation of nature, music, poetry, and food through the medium of Irish

"Only basic Irish is necessary, so I expect a shade of awkwardness during our first grapples with the language.

But that's all right – it'll surface and grow around the right surroundings and people, just like it did for me."

The Kerryman, August 30, 2017.

Ó Cinnéide takes to the field on behalf of his treasured language.

As I've said, some inter-county GAA players I've met have a high opinion of themselves and like to make you feel more nervous than you already are.

Dara Ó Cinnéide does the exact opposite. He was the first man I called when I started with The Kerryman – concerning a Comórtas Peile piece – and I'd no hesitation in meeting him a couple of years later, after he'd landed the role of Munster Regional Manager at Raidió na Gaeltachta.

Aside from being a nice fella, he's also the best footballer never to have won an All-Star. Just saying!

THE captain's acceptance speech does little other than cool the joy supporters feel at winning an All-Ireland. That's because most follow the bland formula favoured by captains throughout the GAA's 133-year history.

For the orator, it's a privilege. For supporters, it's a watery ritual at odds with the fire and colour of All-Ireland day.

Dara Ó Cinnéide spent fewer than five minutes on the Hogan Stand when he accepted Sam Maguire on his county's behalf in 2004 – but for all its brevity, his speech is still revisited by supporters on YouTube each day.

His address could have been especially forgettable; it followed a lifeless All-Ireland final and the re-crowning of a familiar champion – and many couldn't even understand what he had said. Instead, the Baile na hAbha man secured its immortality by delivering it entirely in Corca Dhuibhne Irish. Like Páidí Ó Sé 19 years before him, Ó Cinnéide climbed the Hogan Stand and carried a fading language to the kind of platform it needs but rarely receives.

Now he needs to guide those who're trying to do something similar.

His recent appointment as RTÉ Raidió na Gaeltachta's Munster Regional Manager means Ó Cinnéide must direct a public service for an ever-thinning minority. He's better-equipped than most for the challenge; he has worked at the station since 1999 and previously fronted acclaimed Irish-language programming on RTÉ and TG4.

Equally encouraging is his composure in facing what's ahead. Having taken a gulp of tea in O'Flaherty's bar, Dingle, he fiddles with the yellow wrapper of a Rocky Bar but seems altogether more assured in discussing his future in broadcasting.

"If it's pressure, it's nice pressure," he says as he frees the chocolate from its papery shell. "It's not something I thought about when I started at radio; it just happened over time.

"There are a lot of people who've paid their licence fee and deserve access to a service through their language. When An Ghaeltacht were in the club final in 2004, there were people there from Gaeltachtaí in Donegal, Galway, Waterford, Cork – everywhere. One of the high points of my sporting life was parading before the All-Ireland final in 2000 with Aodán Mac Gearailt, Dara Ó Sé, and Tomás Ó Sé. I looked across to the Galway lads, saw Seán Óg de Paor and Seán Ó Domhnaill, and I thought, 'The Gaeltacht is here'.

"Even when I gave that speech after the All-Ireland in 2004, I saw about 10 rows of Gaeltacht people in the crowd. There's an Irish-speaking public there, and it needs a voice.

"I can't say, 'I want to do x, I want to do y,' because there are always constraints. But I don't want to maintain the status quo, either. I'll protect our impartiality, fluency, and accuracy first. Then, hopefully, people will feel they might miss something if they don't listen to us.

"I'll still broadcast when it's needed. I'll manage services, do housekeeping, and there'll be a need to develop our service throughout Munster. It's not just for Corca Dhuibhne. There are Gaeltachtaí in south Kerry, Cork, and Waterford, and while we all have different personalities and jerseys, we're all on the same team."

But boosting this particular station's visibility is a task hampered by almost unique challenges.

Some Gaeilgeoirí are naively inclined to ignore the English-speaking elephant stomping on their language and pretend all is fine. Their positivity stems from a good place – their thirst for a healthy future for the language is both unquenchable and admirable – but it may not make for the most helpful approach to protecting Gaeilge.

Ó Cinnéide, however, is candid on the language's present-day health and English's ever-growing strength in Gaeltachtaí. He even chuckles at the romantic notion that English was absent from his own youth.

"We also had a good bit of English at home," he says. "Even in the school yards in Scoil Naomh Eirc and Dingle CBS, it was often English we spoke when we were out of earshot. I don't know why – but that's the way it was.

"I didn't think of what it meant to have Irish until I got to third-level education. I left in 1993 for Limerick to study industrial chemistry, and I never heard a word of Irish in my four years in UL.

"But people above there would say 'You speak Irish, don't you?' – and it was then I realised: 'Jaysus, I do!' People from Kerry would tell me they remembered playing football against An Ghaeltacht and that we were a different breed – and that made me proud!

"West Kerry has changed a lot, though. You hear every kind of language now – whereas when I was young, it was Irish nearly all day. That's still true – but there's less now, even west of Dingle.

"Any football team is a reflection of its locality. When I played senior with An Ghaeltacht from 1991 to 2007, there was a small decline in Irish. Today, I don't know if players still set foot on Páirc Caide Ghallarais and think of Irish as one of the club's four pillars. I'm a selector, I'm the PR Officer, I'm every kind of a thing with An Ghaeltacht; it's one of the closest things to my heart – but things are changing."

With the tea now hoovered from his cup, Ó Cinnéide is yet to uncover any light for the language's future. It might be unfair, however, to portray him as defeatist rather than balanced.

"There are always positives," he says as he folds his arms and leans back against the stone wall behind him. "I travel to Dingle every day, and this town is more 'Gaelaí' than it's ever been. There's no shop here that I can't go about my business through Irish.

"I just think we need to put a mirror up to people. You don't have to speak Irish because what you speak, at the end of the day, is an entirely personal choice.

"But I'd like people to realise they have something different and that it's important to protect."

The Kerryman, March 28, 2018.

The book that almost never was

I'm not a history buff, but Brendan McCarthy's work in piecing together the writings of Fr William Ferris was an impressive undertaking. And I'm sure it was worthwhile as Fr Ferris sounds like one of the most interesting figures the Catholic Church in Kerry has seen.

THURSDAY night was the reward for Brendan McCarthy at the end of what has been a laborious process.

It's been six years since he began assembling Fr William Ferris's 'History of the Parishes of BallymacElligott, Ballyseedy, O'Brennan, and Nohoval', which was launched last week by Bishop Ray Browne at Ballygarry House Hotel. When he started, Brendan was looking for something to keep his "grey matter functioning" – and he found it in Tralee Library, home to three boxes of jumbled papers that added up to a completed book.

The process saw him decipher Fr Ferris' handwriting and transcribe his work, which dated back to the 1920s and 1930s. But as the project took shape, new questions arose.

"It had all the things you'd expect in a book: contents, chapters, bibliography, acknowledgements, everything," Brendan told the gathering as evening sunlight filled a dining area at the rear of the hotel. "He even had a list of sellers in Tralee and had lined up *The Kerryman* as publishers. The question I asked, of course, is why this book was never published."

An interest in Ballymacelligott, called home by his forefathers, brought Brendan to his starting point, but this new question triggered the detour that led to this launch.

To give some background, Fr Ferris lived a life of fascinations. The Ratoo-born priest was a brilliant scholar at the Sem and later Maynooth, and he was ordained in 1906, by which time he held both a strong sense of Irish nationalism and a desire for independence. He fell for Irish culture, the Gaelic League, and the Sinn Féin movement, and he even wrote under a pseudonym for a paper led by Arthur Griffith.

Brendan discovered that Fr Ferris lost none of this passion on his return to the Diocese of Kerry, where he spoke at anti-conscription rallies and was a vocal supporter of the War of Independence. His fieriness earned him two death threats from a hit squad; his fearlessness led to the publication of those threats in a newspaper.

"After the treaty, he felt Griffith and Collins had negotiated good terms for the Irish," Brendan explained. "He campaigned for the treaty in Kerry, a brave position given how anti-treaty Kerry was. He did feel the Civil War was a disaster, though, that the country had fallen into a malaise, and he withdrew from the political arena in the early 1920s."

He arrived in Ballymacelligott at the sharp end of that decade, and throughout his curacy, he devoted himself to recording oral history and folklore in danger of going to their holders' graves. As the Priest put it, "Each time the east wind blows, it takes an old seanchaí with it".

After handing out questionnaires at Station Mass breakfasts, Fr Ferris would return to his Presbytery to put order on the bounties. The tirelessness of his work would not make it immune to pitfalls, however; following protocol, he submitted his work to Bishop Michael O'Brien – who delivered an uppercut to the project.

"He [Fr Ferris] was shocked some weeks later to receive a letter saying publication was prohibited," Brendan explained, "because he had claimed that Saint Brendan was born in Ballymacelligott. Adopted Diocese tradition at the time said he was born in Fenit and Baptised in Ardfert."

An alteration could have saved the project from its 80-or-so years in the archives of UCC's Boole Library and, later, the County Library in Tralee – but, unmoved by authority, Fr Ferris was not for turning.

He was a man, after all, who told the people that rugby, not Gaelic football, was the true successor to the

ancient game of caid. He was a maverick who construct-
ed a more digestible form of The 10 Commandments for
his Parishioners: 'six things to do and six things not to
do'. A rewrite, naturally, never materialised.

"Shortly after the rejection – but not as a result of this,
as far as I can tell – he was moved to Millstreet, where
he started to write the history of that parish," Brendan
said. "This time, he used a pseudonym, so he didn't have
to submit his work again."

Through his editing and research, Brendan feels that
he got to know the man a little – though not a lot.

It seems curious that Fr Ferris's project was saved by
someone he never met. It's similarly curious, and wonderful, to see Bishop Ray Browne taking to the micro-
phone to offer the work its official launch in 2018 – 47
years after Fr Ferris's death at age 91.

"I think we're making a tiny bit of history here tonight with the current Bishop of Kerry launching the
same book that his predecessor banned 85 years ago,"
Brendan said, prompting chuckles from his audience. "In
a certain sense, I think it closes the circle which began all
those years ago."

The Kerryman, June 13, 2018.

Living the Blasket life

I'd never visited the Blaskets – much to my shame as a west Kerry man – until I met Lesley Kehoe and Gordon Bond in 2019. They were working there as caretakers and would spend an entire summer on the island.

It's the only time I've taken a boat to an interview, and I left feeling rather jealous of the couple as our boat moved away; the weather was gorgeous, and if there's a more beautiful place on earth than An Blascaod Mór on a fine day, please take me there.

COM Dhíneol and the mainland are only kilometres away, and America is the nearest parish to the west. But the sights, sounds, and fauna of An Blascaod Mór would have you believe heaven is closer than either.

Imagine living and working on the island as Lesley Kehoe and Gordon Bond are, tending to a hostel once home to Peig Sayers, greeting visitors and selling teas and coffees from a building once home to Micheál Ó Catháin.

Imagine waking up to the view of grey seals rolling on the sand of An Trá Bán, of Arctic Terns settling on nearby Beiginis.

It's an experience few have had since the island's evacuation in 1953, but it's been part of their life for a month. It'll be that way until autumn.

"We were both commuting to Dublin from Kildare. I left home at 7am and got home at 7pm, and four hours each day were taken up by the commute," Lesley says at a timber picnic table adjacent to the island shop.

"I was in the heritage sector, working in the 'Seamus Heaney: Listen Now Again' exhibition. Gordon was in the civil service. I loved my job, I love Heaney, but the commute does drain you after a while.

"I was on Facebook on the train home from work one evening when I came across this post looking for someone to look after the hostel and shop for the summer. I got off the train, sat into my car, and rang the people who put the post up – Billy O'Connor and Alice Hayes – and two weeks later, we met them."

"On February 10, we were told the job was ours," Gordon says. "We've been here nearly a month, and we still can't believe we're sitting here."

The transition from life in the Dublin area to life on an island that feels a world removed from west Kerry, never mind our largest city, is as ragged as the cliffs skirting Na Blascaodaí.

Billy O'Connor ferries visitors over from Dingle Marina most days, weather permitting. He also brings the essentials to Gordon and Lesley.

The couple stay overnight in a room upstairs from the island shop. Their water comes from a spring. There's no electricity, of course not, and they rely on gas for cooking. Timber and coal fuel a stove in the house, but it doesn't kill the chill.

"What gets you [in relation to heat] is when the light fades in the evening," Gordon says. "We're so busy with all the visitors coming in that you keep moving, and you don't get cold. But when the light is fading, the houses have small windows, you have to open the half door, and then the wind whips around. But it's a case, really, of throwing on another jumper.

"The weather changes so quickly. Today it's beautiful, but on another day, you can't even see the coastline, never mind Dún Chaoin."

"But there's beauty in that as well, and it's a privilege to be able to see the place when it's like that, when this huge wind comes at it," Lesley says. "When the weather is bad, no visitors come out by boat, so very few people get to experience what we experience."

The island hasn't had a community for almost 70 years, but it lives on regardless. Tourists are today treading its neatly mown walkways. There isn't much by way of chatting between the visitors, but rather than being glued to phones, they're transfixed by the views, the greenery, the animals, the buildings, the ruins.

People make hostel bookings months in advance, Lesley explains. One woman is here studying the seals, while Lesley's parents have gone off for a walk as their two-day visit to the island nears its end. It is a quiet place now, but it still has energy.

"It still has this vibrant life that's been going on since 1953," Lesley says. "We're hearing more and more stories. You've had scholars coming over ever since, and you hear about how former islanders came over on day trips.

"We came here first in 2017, while I was writing a dissertation on the Blaskets' intangible heritage. But even we are learning something new every day. Like how the islanders couldn't get their heads around the new two-storey buildings that were being built here in the 1910s. They couldn't understand why someone 'would build a house on top of another house'.

"Gordon was fortunate in that he could take a career break to do this. I left my job, but I don't feel like I've left the heritage sector. Even though it's a case of minding a hostel and a shop, I still feel like it's a heritage job."

"Even a woman was here today telling us how she came over here in her teens for two weeks on co-op, and you had football matches on the beach," Gordon says. "We're learning more and more about its afterlife.

"We're not really thinking about the transition back to the mainland right now. We have to soak this up. It'll be a tough experience to match. But I suppose we'll just have to ease ourselves back into everyday life slowly. I'd guess we won't be back to the 7am commute right away!"

A few hours later, the visitors board Billy's boat, and the chatter among them is of how the visit trumped even their lofty expectations.

As the motor noises and the boat sets off on the hour-long journey to Dingle, Lesley's parents – Gaye and Noel – wave from the deck; Lesley and Gordon wave back from the island.

It's not as painful a departure as the ones made by the island's former inhabitants setting off for mainland life before 1953. But it's poignant all the same.

Some things never change around here.

The Kerryman, May 1, 2019.

Part Three

Fighting the Odds

No stopping Christy's comeback

I vaguely remember hearing about Adrian 'Christy' O'Connor's accident in London around the time it happened, in 2004, and I knew that he had run many marathons and half-marathons since then.

What I didn't know before meeting him was that doctors felt his brain injury would probably prevent him from walking again, let alone running. As comebacks go, his was extraordinary.

ADRIAN 'Christy' O'Connor's comeback didn't merely defy medical predictions; it blew them asunder.

He'd likely never walk or talk again, he was told after sustaining a brain injury in London in late 2004; he has since finished three full marathons and is closing in on his 10th half marathon. 'Christy's Come Back' is a modest title for his freshly published memoirs, that most extraordinary of contexts considered.

"In December 2004, I was over in England for a wedding party, the wedding of two of my friends," he says of the day his life took its detour. "There was a gang of us on the way back from a nightclub, and we were doing the usual messing you have after nights out. We found an old chair with wheels, and we started pushing each other around in it, you know yourself.

"When it was my go to hop up on the chair, I ran away and tripped over a small wall. I fell, and the right-hand side of my skull hit the pavement."

The Clochán man suffered a traumatic brain injury and was placed in an induced coma. His survival was no certainty; his odds of walking and talking again were slimmer still.

"But that wasn't the end of me, and that's the message I want to get out there to people," he says. "A brain injury doesn't have to be the end of the road. You can still have a good life. I did."

We're sitting at the bar in Dingle's Skellig Hotel this Monday morning, two days after he launched his first book in O'Connor's Bar in his native parish. On the night of the launch, *The Kerryman* called out to Clochán after Adrian agreed to an interview. Alas, we hadn't accounted for his popularity, which became hearteningly clear upon entering O'Connor's.

While a dark, damp night took hold of a parish at the toes of Mount Brandon, dozens of people, perhaps a few hundred, took cover in the homely Clochán bar, and a queue snaked through the sky-blue room to the table at which Adrian was seated. As he penned his signature to each copy, the assembly of well-wishers seemed to gain new recruits by the second.

It was going to be some time before he'd get away from his task. With that, this writer tapped him on the shoulder and told him we'd leave the interview for a couple of days and to enjoy his night.

From a reporter's point of view, that kind of move comes with the risk of missing the moment. But as he polishes off a coffee in the Skellig this morning, the enthusiasm Adrian showed in addressing the many people who attended his book launch hasn't dimmed in the days since passed.

"This is a happy story," he says. "The accident is only a small part of this book. What I've done since is a much bigger part of it.

"The journey back was a 'bóthar fada' for me – but I made it. As you can see on the front of the book, running is a big part of my life now. That picture was taken when I did the Dublin Marathon in 2008; that was my first one, and I did two more after that.

"The Dingle Marathon in 2010 took me a long while, though; I was more than 10 hours on the road. Since 2011, it's been the half marathon in Dingle every year. I'm already getting things sorted for 2019."

Comebacks such as his don't take hours, days, or weeks. His life, for some time, spun from University Hospital Kerry to Cork University Hospital to the National Rehabilitation Hospital in Dún Laoghaire; from tube-feedings to operations to times spent in a wheelchair.

It wasn't until October 2006 that he walked unsupported again. That moment arrived on Fermoyle beach, around 10 metres from his brother's car, after he set his tripod aside and tried what most of us have taken as given since we were toddlers.

He made it back to the car that day, and his determination has taken him still further since.

"Running to Castlegregory from my home, that's 10.5 kilometres – so I've a half-marathon done there," he says. "Usually on Saturdays, when the weather is good, I'll do it. But, as you know yourself, you often don't get good weather in west Kerry. Whenever I want, though, I'll go and do it.

"I picked up qualifications from the National Learning Network and Tralee Community College, but those marathons and half marathons – and this book – are my proudest achievements. And when I have my 10th half marathon done, I'll go back and do a 'full' again."

His book tells a largely happy story, as the 42-year-old words it himself – but he has regrets. In 2004, he was in the second year of his Civil Engineering studies at UCC and was living with his then-girlfriend. He never graduated from that course, and he feels his chance at marriage has passed by. He cannot drive, and while his love of GAA didn't fade, he never togged out to cross the white lines again.

That said, the accident also brought him experiences he'd have never enjoyed otherwise.

"I'd probably have never had written for local media or have been written about in local and national media," he says. "And I'm certain I'd have never picked up an award at the Dingle People of the Year Awards in 2015.

"I have regrets, and there are things I can't do. But there are things I can do, too. I've found things that make me happy; I've finished marathons, and now I'm a writer – I'm in the same territory as Con Dennehy and Enid Blyton!

"The medics said I'd never walk or talk again; well, they were so bloody wrong."

The Kerryman, November 14, 2018.

'I spoke out – and that saved my life.'

When he spoke out about his depression in late 2018, Eoghan Ó Conchúir did a favour for everyone who has suffered from that terrible illness. I suppose it has touched all of us at some point in some way, but it's thanks to people such as Eoghan that we feel comfortable talking about it.

AMONG the most recent interviews to appear on *The Kerryman*'s pages looked into the story of Clochán's Adrian O'Connor, a young man who sustained a brain injury in London 14 years ago and was given little hope of survival, let alone of walking or talking again.

Roll forward 10 half marathons and one full marathon, and it would be the height of understatement to say he confounded medical predictions.

Eoghan Ó Conchúir – affectionately known as 'Clais' locally, in reference to his home townland in the Feothanach area – wasn't the first to gain inspiration from the Clochán man, but few felt as empowered by Adrian's story as he did.

While giving Adrian a lift over the Conor Pass to Dingle, the 30-year-old listened to and talked to a man with an almost unique story.

In the months leading up to this encounter, Eoghan had battled and taken control of depression, an illness that nearly claimed his life. Today, Eoghan sits in Dingle's Benners Hotel, knowing that tens of thousands have listened to his call on Facebook for people to ignore the stigma that sometimes goes with depression and take steps like those that saved him last summer.

"Adrian wasn't given much hope by his medics – and he's done a marathon since, a few half marathons. It's inspirational," Eoghan says as he pours some brown sugar into a "badly wanted" cup of coffee. "I have my second chance, too, and meeting Adrian spurred me to do the Facebook video. I'm not doing it for myself but for those afraid to speak out."

For all the evidence that proves depression isn't picky when selecting those it chases down, the last traces of stigma have clung on as stickily as the illness itself. Eoghan is further living proof that achievements in work and life don't provide immunity from depression.

Married to Mary and living with their 10-month-old son in Brandon, a gem on the north of the Corca Dhuibhne peninsula, Eoghan isn't short of home comforts. He also worked as a healthcare assistant and recently qualified as a Special Needs Assistant, further evidence that 'the boy's done good'.

The same could be said of the many men and women Eoghan met following his admission to University Hospital Kerry (UHK) last summer. Over those three weeks, Eoghan got to know people of all professions, aged from 18 to 90 – and this is a big part of what he's trying to drill home: depression, he feels, is something most people suffer with at some point.

Though initially "a small bit embarrassed", Eoghan found the courage last June to speak to loved ones and take his first steps towards days that are "average to good, most of the time". It's what he needed to do to pin down an illness that had gnawed away at his sleep; left him with constant pressure headaches; put a shake in his knee that "could have lifted a cavity block"; and had him thinking of leaving this world long before his time.

"I take some medication, but the main difference now is that I keep life simple. It's hard, sometimes, with a 10-month-old baby, Micheál, but I like to have my day planned out," he says. "I take 20 minutes for myself every day: I put away the phone, go for a walk, take in some fresh air – it cleans my mind.

"But I was lucky because I spoke out. We all know in every village, every town in Kerry, the country, it has affected people. Maybe some people were afraid to speak out, and they're not around now. The stigma that's there is causing harm.

"I spoke out, and that was what saved my life; by that June bank holiday weekend, when I broke down with my wife, Mary, and my sister, Niamh, I felt it was a case of either speaking out or I was going to consider suicide.

"I just thought I could manage it myself but, when I look back now, there's no way I could have done that… What I did was like putting an egg into a frying pan in December and leaving it there until June. My brain was cremated by summer."

With that single move – opening up to two people he loves and trusts – months of pressure began to melt away.

It hadn't been long since Mary and Eoghan had moved from Dublin, where he had buried himself in work, often following his day's labour with night classes as he pursued his goal of becoming an SNA. But rural life isn't without its tests either. As the long winter had its say last year, animals starved on fodderless farms nationwide. Eoghan helps out on the family farm in Feothanach, and while his flock of 120 sheep made it through the crisis, he admits the stories and images that dominated the 2018 farming year shook him.

By the time the frost and snow gave way to the rainless weeks of last summer, there wasn't a budge from the grass, but sheep prices plunged. Such events are never welcome, but they become all the more serious when you're looking after a baby at home.

These stresses were part of what led to a three-week stay in UHK, but aside from the heartache of facing up to visits from Mikey, his "leasainm" for little Micheál, Eoghan never doubted he was in the right place to get better – and any embarrassment he once felt because of his illness had melted by the time he took to Facebook in December.

"I said in the video to speak out to someone you love and someone you trust, but your doctors and good charities like Pieta House or AWARE are also there," he says. "Along with my family in Brandon and Feothanach, I owe a lot to the medical people in UHK, too; I can't thank them enough.

"When I rang SouthDoc on the June bank holiday, there were no beds for me until the following Tuesday, but that's not the medics' fault, that's the fellas in the suits and ties, even though it's the people working on the ground that are down with it. It's a thankless job, really.

"You never hear a good word about them – but I'm saying right now that they were brilliant to me. I just hope that people will listen now to my video and try to get the help I got."

The Kerryman, January 9, 2019.
Farming Independent, January 12, 2019.

Jack and Jill helped Hannah climb that hill.

This was my third time interviewing the Falvey family from Annascaul, and this was the best visit of the three, I reckon.

You see, Nancy and Brendan's youngest daughter, Hannah, suffers from Rett Syndrome and will never talk. The odds of her walking were slim too – but on the Saturday morning on which I carried out this interview, I did see her walking. That was special.

MUCH has changed for Hannah Falvey over the past three years, mostly for the better.

Some parts of her life remain as they were when *The Kerryman* called in to Annascaul in mid-2016, but that's no bad thing. Her smile is as lovely now as it was then, and her chuckle's no less hearty.

She still has that wonder in her eyes, the kind that won our hearts three years ago. Due to Rett syndrome, she can't talk, can't tell us the little stories most five-year-olds love to share – but her eyes and her laughter are expressive enough to fill that void.

And the things that have changed in the interim can mostly be chalked down as positives. A few are small steps, some literally, in the right direction; others are a touch more trivial.

"She still loves Peppa Pig," dad Brendan jokes, "but she's more into Mr Tumble now. He comes on in the morning on the BBC kids' channel. When she's in another room and she hears Mr Tumble noising from the sitting room telly, she starts roaring laughing. You love Mr Tumble, don't you, Hannah?"

Her eyes lock on Dad's; that'd be a yes.

But the real progress – notable, uplifting victories over the brain disorder she was diagnosed as having in 2015 – lies elsewhere.

Her routine today includes pre-school, three weekdays of which are spent in a mainstream school in Camp. She's set for further adventure in September as the nearest primary school, Scoil Bhreac Chluain in Annascaul village, prepares to welcome Hannah.

Three years ago, Brendan and Nancy (Hannah's mom) were hopeful a Tobii screen, operated by eye movements, would give their girl some means of communication; those with Rett syndrome never speak, one of the brain disorder's many miseries.

No sooner has Nancy set up the screen today when beep after beep flows from the device, each prompted by Hannah's eye movements. She's engrossed in a game, and her chuckling suggests she's playing a blinder.

"The Tobii screen takes a bit of practice, but Hannah is now very precise," Nancy says.

"We mainly got it for her education, so it's going to play an even bigger role from here. She's already going to pre-school, and the screen can be set up according to the lessons of the day. This will continue in primary school.

"At the moment, we use it mainly at feeding time. It's her means of telling us what she'd like to eat. But education was mainly what we had in mind from day one."

But it's after her nurse, Niamh, cleans bits of creamy pancake from Hannah's chin that the Annascaul girl prepares to show us the best of her new skills.

After Nancy lifts her from her high chair, she holds Hannah's hands in hers and helps her find her footing. Without the aid of her splints, Hannah plants her feet on the timber floor; her legs are as straight and firm as posts.

As Mom keeps a tender grip on her hands, Hannah takes one step, then another.

There's a thud with each step, seven or eight in all. The clap of her shoes against the timber floor is as lively from her weaker right foot as it is from her left, a happy surprise even to Brendan and Nancy. She covers roughly two metres, but the progress of recent years is apparent even on a journey as short as this one.

"She definitely hasn't gone backwards," Brendan says of the past three years.

"She was in and out of hospital quite often between things like reflux and chest infections, but that has changed. She hasn't been in at all in the last two years.

"Her footing is good, and we also have a special tricycle. She sits up on it, we push her along, and we're trying to get her pedalling. It's more exercise for her, it builds up her leg movements, and she loves being out and about and meeting people in the village. A sunny day like today is ideal for it."

It's unlikely these steps, impressive and strong though they are, will develop into independent walking. Nancy can't see it.

But they're the product of intense physio work, and they're sources of pride and signs of progress.

They're also testament to Brendan and Nancy's hard work and the sterling assistance they've received up to this point.

The HSE continues to help Hannah – thus helping Brendan, Nancy, and Hannah's big sister, Lily, in the process – by providing her with 22 crucial hours' nursing a week: 18 through Resistance Ireland and another four directly.

But before Hannah turned five, The Jack and Jill Children's Foundation provided the funding the Falveys needed to get Hannah to this point. The family started with a carer and later turned to nursing but, all in all, were able to avail of 40 hours' assistance each month.

"She definitely wouldn't be as strong as she is today," Nancy says.

"She's in the third of the four phases of the syndrome at the moment, the plateau, during which you can make gains with intense intervention. The next phase, a regression phase, usually comes between 10 and 12, with motor deterioration.

"But there are physio experts in Israel who believe you can avoid or milden this with early, intense intervention. 'Jack and Jill' helped Brendan and I do what we could never have done on our own.

"During our time with them, they were able to help a child up to the age of five, whereas previously it had been up to four. That was a huge boost to us and made the transition [to life after Jack and Jill] that bit easier.

"Without them, she certainly wouldn't have been able to stand like she does now. But it wasn't just that; it was respite for us.

"They read her stories and helped with feeding – which can take 30 to 40 minutes. They showered and bathed her, they gave me medical advice, they got her using her Tobii screen more often.

"They were quick, there was no bureaucracy, no fighting for hours. They put in the groundwork up to the age of five, which Niamh here and the HSE have since continued.

"I would like to sum it up in one sentence what Jack and Jill helped us do – but I can't."

"We were in dire straits after the diagnosis – but once we had that diagnosis and made contact with Jack and Jill, a supervisor came in here and told us the diagnosis was all we needed," Brendan says. "In our hour of need with a sick child, they were there."

The Kerryman, March 27, 2019.

Helping little Alexis reach
her potential

A short time after meeting Hannah Falvey once again, I met another family who'd benefitted from the help of the Jack and Jill Foundation: the O'Mahonys of Woodlawn, Killarney.

Young Alexis O'Mahony has a severely debilitating genetic condition, and I'd written about her struggles before, but this was my first time meeting her in person. And, once again, I was left in awe at what parents will do for those they love most.

IF the day you take your first steps isn't the most important of your life, it ranks highly.

You take one step, then another. They coax smiles and cheers from those around you. But the excitement melts away quickly. Walking is taken as a given from very early on.

For someone living with a genetic condition such as PDH deficiency, your family will celebrate your first steps for as long as they live. Alexis O'Mahony is three years old and hasn't taken her first steps yet. It may take another few years. It may never happen.

141

She can move herself from one part of a room to another. Her dad, Steve O'Mahony, shows a video of his girl, face down, using her arms to push herself, backwards, around their sitting-room floor in Killarney's Woodlawn.

The process is slow. For a viewer, it's at once upsetting and uplifting. Upsetting because she can't yet do what most three-year-olds do so naturally; upsetting because it reminds one she has already faced having Cerebral Palsy, poor muscle tone, dislocated hips, and acute feeding difficulties.

Uplifting because it shows grit, and her awareness that she has the power to move; uplifting because it's a small victory over a life-limiting condition.

"Anything is possible," Steve says. "Maybe she'll take two or three steps when she's 10. Maybe she'll never walk. But there's no point thinking about that. My wife Teresa and I, and all the people helping Alexis, are just focussed on her reaching her potential, whatever it may be. What she's doing now, pushing herself around, might not have been possible before. It shows she has energy and fight, and awareness that she has this power.

"Her sight has improved. Because of having PDH deficiency, she has a brain abnormality that affects her eyes. Before, she would never make eye contact. Now she recognises some people, some shapes and colours.

"With a cortical vision impairment, there is scope for improvement, and a lot of work has been put in by people to achieve that. And because she now recognises some shapes, some colours, it gives her motivation to move towards those things."

"One of the people helping us with her vision found that Alexis only recognises the colour red," mom Teresa says. "In the past few weeks, Alexis has started to recognise purple. That, for us, is a huge thing."

With evening slowly turning to night outside, bright orange salt lamps light the room. The rattle of windchimes, a huge hit with Alexis, billows from a recording Steve has on his phone. Every part of the ambience is designed to stimulate Alexis' brain.

PDH deficiency is a metabolic disease that makes it difficult to break down nutrients in food; it's characterised by a range of neurological problems and lactic-acid build-up.

Through peg-feeding, Alexis nowadays receives a precise ketogenic diet – high in fat and free of carbohydrates – to control her epilepsy. The garage adjoined to their home is loaded with equipment needed to help Alexis reach her potential.

To be truthful, it's hard to keep tabs on all the information the couple shares about Alexis and her fight.

It shows that day-to-day life is hugely challenging, certainly. But it's just as clear that her parents' attention to detail is pinpoint, a testament to their love for Alexis and their commitment to helping her.

Signs of progress are there, and they're impressive. During the first 16 months of her life, Alexis made 12 trips to Temple Street Hospital, the centre-point of her treatment. These days, she can often go the maximum three months between her week-long stays.

The family hasn't done it alone as such a thing would require strength beyond the remarkable. In the past week alone, the O'Mahonys have received assistance from the Kerry Intervention and Disability Services (KIDS); a physiotherapist in Farranfore; Enable Ireland; Resistance Ireland; a public-health nurse; and a Clinical Nurse Consultant.

"That wouldn't even cover everyone," Steve says.

The focal point in keeping touch with day-to-day normality, a source of 10 hours' respite a week, is the 'Jack and Jill Children's Foundation'.

With the foundation's assistance, the couple can zone in on the mundane but necessary tasks that make up everyday life, in the comfort of knowing a nurse is taking care of Alexis.

"I think Alexis is one of 11 children in Kerry that 'Jack and Jill' are helping, and when they're here, 40 hours a month, Teresa and I can go to the pharmacy for Alexis, we can get equipment we need from KIDS," Steve says. "We can also cut the lawn, make the dinner, whatever we need to do around the home. Two nurses are currently splitting the hours between them, and they're a lifeline to us.

"We always wanted to give something back to them, like we did for Temple Street before. With her birthday coming up, we decided to kill two birds with one stone."

From 2pm to 5pm on Good Friday (April 19), grown-ups and kids alike will immerse themselves in a world of wonder at the Dromhall Hotel in Killarney. For the kids, there'll be face-painting; balloon-modelling; gymnastics and cheer-leading; Easter egg hunts; and yoga sessions. For the bigger kids, scones, cakes, teas, and coffees await between the holistic and beauty therapies on offer. 'Alexis's Third Birthday Bash' will be a party worthy of a special person and a foundation that supports her family so thoroughly.

"It's an idea I came up with, and the owner of Peak Performance Gym – Bobby Enright – and Siobhan Reen from 'Jack and Jill Kerry' have been heavily involved," Steve says. "Bobby will also be running gym challenges in Peak Performance the same day.

"People sometimes buy Alexis toys, but because of her condition, they often don't get used. So, instead, people can donate to 'Jack and Jill' on the day. What they give, no matter how small, will help children like Alexis, wherever in the country those children may be. As little as €16 covers an hour's nursing for a child."

The Kerryman, April 10, 2019.

Breaking electoral barriers

I don't need much of an intro to this piece about Lios Póil man Micheál Kelliher because it's written in the 'first person'; the article is the intro, effectively. It's nice that it stands out, in a way, just as Micheál himself did in 2019.

IT may be clichéd to describe someone as a history-maker – but Micheál Kelliher genuinely has made history.

He did so by becoming the first Deaf person to put himself forward for local election – or any election in this country, for that matter.

And if the Independents4Change candidate convinces enough people in Cabra-Glasnevin that he's the best person to represent them, he'll create further history by becoming Ireland's first Deaf Councillor.

This piece is no attempt to boost the fortunes of a party that – according to a March 7 Ipsos/MRBI poll – has the support of just two per cent of people in Dublin.

What we can do is give you an idea of the kind of person Micheál is.

Though we're both from Lios Póil, he's four years my senior, and with him being Deaf, we never attended the same school. We, therefore, had little to do with each other.

My grandfather gave many years coaching local draughts teams and regarded Micheál as the best young player he'd seen. That was as much as I knew about him until very recently.

"No, no," Micheál says this afternoon in Cam an Lóndraigh. "There were better players than me on my team, never mind the other teams."

My grandfather also describes him as "an absolute gentleman". Going by Micheál's modest appraisal of his draughts-playing abilities, 'Granda' might be right.

Getting away from Lios Póil's early noughties draughts scene and on to more current and pressing matters, it's important to understand why Micheál is running for election and why he's doing so in Dublin rather than Kerry.

Cam an Lóndraigh is like many townlands in this county and country. For a stranger to get there, they've to solve a riddle of bóithríns.

It's less isolated than most townlands; thriving Dingle is only a 10-minute journey away. But it's pretty bloody isolated all the same, and if you're Deaf, that remoteness feels keener still.

"It was tough growing up Deaf in west Kerry," Micheál says.

"I only know four others here [the Dingle Peninsula] who are Deaf. Before I was 12, I went to school in

Presentation Primary in Tralee. It's an all-girls school, but it had a Deaf unit. After that, I went to St Joseph's School for Deaf Boys in Cabra. I could have gone to Mounthawk, but I would have been one of just four [Deaf] students.

"St Joseph's had 85 students, and you have a much bigger Deaf community locally, around 5,000 people. I'm still in north Dublin now."

Going about everyday matters is challenging when you're Deaf. Being Deaf and running for election brings these challenges into sharper focus; you can't succeed in politics if you can't communicate with the electorate.

The process of this very interview isn't straightforward. I put questions to Micheál, and his girlfriend, Lauri, 'signs' them.

It's a smooth-enough system, and it helps that Micheál's verbal skills are strong, but the interview does move at a slower pace than what I'm used to. It's also slower than what the people he's campaigning to are used to when politicians come to their door.

When the means to clear such hurdles aren't available, campaigning depends on others' goodwill.

"An interpreter costs about €600 a day, and you need two interpreters," Micheál says.

"Earlier this year, Clare Daly asked Minister John Paul Phelan if there were plans for a pilot scheme, like one in the UK, to provide candidates who have disabilities with financial support for disability-related costs. There weren't.

"I'm lucky to have a great team of volunteers behind me. Without them, this would be very costly."

It's unsurprising to learn that matters affecting Deaf people and those with disabilities are at the heart of his campaign, though his manifesto covers more issues than just these. After all, it was being at the forefront of the Right2Water and 'Together for Yes' campaigns that piqued his interest in politics.

On the former point, Micheál feels things have improved for Deaf people during his lifetime – but not enough, and certainly not quickly enough.

Before finding work as a civil engineer and later a software engineer, he says some companies wouldn't take him on because he was Deaf.

He can't carry out some tasks; that much is true. But when a work colleague takes a call on his behalf, he can fill in elsewhere for his colleague, perhaps by answering some e-mails, he explains. That seems a fair point to me.

A private college refused to provide a sign-language interpreter for him when he needed it. Some private transport companies have not accepted his free-travel pass.

He has frequently criticised what he feels is RTÉ's cynical attitude towards Irish Sign Language [ISL]. The national broadcaster only showed the ISL version of the national anthem for a few seconds before last year's All-Ireland hurling final. This, in his opinion, was one example of RTÉ's disrespect towards the language.

Everything considered, he feels the Deaf community remains extremely marginalised, and he's working with 'Unite the Union' to set up a branch supporting the Deaf community.

"Things have improved and are improving," he says. "But it's happening too slowly. The Irish Sign Language Bill was signed into law in 2017, but we still don't have full implementation. Very few children have access to ISL. Not all public services provide access to ISL.

"I think my campaign has energised the Deaf community, and I'm getting a good reaction from the wider public as well because my campaign is not just based on Deaf rights.

"I want public housing for all, where the rent would be based on people's income, not a building's value. I want public services based on human rights, not on pockets. I want public transport to be more accessible for wheelchair users and free to use for everyone [as it is in Tallinn and Dunkirk]. I want to penalise companies for non-sustainable environmental practices.

"What appeals to me about Independents4Change is that it is based on human rights – not your pocket."

I don't know if Micheál will win a Council seat in May, and I can't tell anyone reading in Dublin to vote for him.

What I can confirm, as he waves me goodbye this afternoon, is that Granda was right. He is a gentleman.

The Kerryman, March 20, 2019.

Note: Micheál did not fare well on polling day and was among the first candidates eliminated from the contest. None of that, however, overshadows the fact that he had broken a sizeable electoral barrier just by running.

Still smiling, still inspiring

Since he was injured terribly in a cycling accident in 2017, I've often asked myself how I'd have reacted if I were in Ian O'Connell's position. The answer: with nowhere near as much dignity as he has shown. He was just 16 when that accident happened, and the consequences were dreadful.

I think the entire county has been nothing less than inspired by his attitude to life in spite of what happened to him.

IAN O'Connell was only 16 when a cycling accident at Killarney National Park forced him onto a wheelchair. While his injuries weren't life-ending, they were life-limiting and, given his tender age, could've easily been life-defining.

But inner strength matched by love and backing from family, friends, and community is a powerful thing. Ian would love to go back to August 2017 and send his life along a different course, but he has also learned that even the most dreadful situations can lead to some good.

He had a choice, as he puts it himself: he could've kept asking 'Why me?' but instead asked 'Why not me?'

"I was in hospital, and I saw how bad the situation was," the Spa clubman tells *The Kerryman* in Killarney's Great Southern Hotel, just hours after receiving a Civic Reception, the Council's highest honour. "They were telling me the extent of my injuries, and I had my choice then.

"I was either going to leave it get to me and feel sorry for myself, or use it to motivate others and help others."

He pursued the latter and made a success of that. Even during this relatively short interview, three people step in at different times to congratulate Ian on his Civic Reception, bestowed upon him for "his courage and positive attitude in the face of adversity". Among his well-wishers is Independent Councillor Charlie Farrelly, who tells him he's "a right inspiration".

"That's what pushes me," Ian says after Cllr Farrelly's kind words. "It's then you realise you're touching people with your story…It means a lot."

Since confounding some dire predictions – it was initially thought he could be on a ventilator for life, but he came off it within 80 days – and a nine-month hospital spell, Ian has become well-known to the public through newspaper, radio, and television appearances, not least via his own podcast and a superb interview on the grand-daddy of Irish shows, the Late Late.

He's now in Leaving Cert year in St Brendan's College, and it won't cause even the mildest surprise to hear he's eyeing up a career in radio broadcasting after this summer's exams.

His situation has brought into focus challenges in everyday life that, understandably, he hadn't noticed before autumn 2017. Some of these have cropped up in his studies. But, as his way, he doesn't make a whole lot of them.

"On my computer, they've a lot of technology and stuff so, I've this thing, you speak and it will just type it out," he says of his Leaving Cert preparations.

"Technology is getting so good now these days; it makes life so easy.

"But there are some small things [that can pose challenges]. It's only when you're in a wheelchair that you notice things, like accessibility on footpaths, cars parked with two wheels up on the footpath. You can't pass then.

"As I say, they're small things, and I don't want to be giving out about them, but it's only when you're in this situation – it's eye-opening."

When asked about his physical condition, he looks down at his arm: "My left hand, I can lift it up a bit," he says, hovering it inches above his wheelchair armrest.

It may be a movement that most take as a given but, for Ian, it is, of course, a spectacular success.

"Unbelievable [the day he could move his hand again]. It's crazy that, when they didn't give me much of a chance…you realise that the physio and stuff is paying off. It makes you try harder and harder again.

"I'm doing physio every day. I've done as much as I can. I go to Cork twice a week for intense weight physio.

I'm putting in the work, and it's paying off. Hopefully, I can get the two hands back. That's the aim.

"Mentally, I'm fully in focus, blinkers going straight. I'm feeling good in myself as well, like; stronger and healthier."

It's late of a Friday, and tomorrow night Ian will travel to Dublin for Bellator 240, a Mixed Martial Arts event, at which he's hoping to meet, once again, the world's most divisive sports star: Conor McGregor. 'The Notorious' has alienated more and more of the Irish public in recent times but, to his ever-diminishing credit, maintains contact with Ian through Instagram, the 18-year-old explains.

McGregor is part of an ever-lengthening roll-call of celebrities to have met and felt impressed by Ian. It's a list that also includes Michael Fassbender and former world darts champion Gary Anderson.

Ian can't stand up, but he has stood out – with more than a little help from those a little closer to home than Anderson or McGregor.

"The support I've received since the accident is second to none," he says. "It's unreal how people can rally together when something bad happens in the community. Family and friends have been there since day one. I can't thank them enough and, every day, more and more people are rowing in behind me.

"I'm going to keep going and try as hard as I can for them."

The Kerryman, February 26, 2020.

155

Céad Míle Fáilte?

I remembered hearing of the racist abuse Úna-Minh Kavanagh suffered in Dublin one day in 2013. I didn't know then that it wasn't a lone incident – just the most shocking one.

She's a Tralee woman, and that's where she launched her memoir, 'Anseo', in 2019. It's a cracking read – I finished it in just two sittings – and by the end of it, I was dying to meet the writer, who agreed to call into our office on Denny Street the following day.

ON an early summer's day in 2013, 21-year-old Úna-Minh Kavanagh stood on Dublin's Parnell Street when a boy, part of a group of some 10 teenagers, called her "a f***ing ch*nk". He grabbed her face and spat on her.

As Úna-Minh wiped his spit from her hair and skin, the boy and his friends laughed and walked away. Nobody on the street stopped to comfort the Tralee woman.

In her new memoir, Anseo, her account of this incident makes for her book's most powerful section. But this moment and other encounters with racism – online or offline, 'casual' or more 'direct' – fall short of defining her story.

After being adopted from a Vietnamese hospital 28 years ago, Úna-Minh spent a wonderful childhood in Tralee with her mother, Noreen, and grandad, Paddy, and indeed she found it harder to write about her grandad's death than about the ugliness she has faced on Parnell Street and elsewhere.

"I had addressed it [Paddy's death] at the time in 2006 and had gone through the process – but now I had to go back and do every step of what happened that day," she tells *The Kerryman* of writing about the Baile na nGall man, who served as a Garda in Tralee from 1949 onwards.

"I had to go through the motions of rereading his appreciation, talking to my Mom about it, talking to my cousins about it, and how everyone was dealing with it – because I know I wasn't dealing with it at the time.

"He deserved a book about him. I'm so sad that nobody came to him and got his story down properly – so I'm happy that I at least have some chunk of him here."

Paddy's influence on her life and her book will be apparent even to those who won't turn to page one. The cover shows him sitting on a grassy ditch – set against a typically scenic Corca Dhuibhne background – and he's a picture of happiness with his arm around his grand-daughter. Úna-Minh proudly sports his caipín, and her smile's exactly as wide as grandad's.

It was Úna-Minh's mother, Noreen, who captured the moment.

In 1991, Noreen travelled to Bach Mai Hospital in Hanoi, Vietnam, as a single woman with dreams of motherhood. Úna-Minh – whose birth-mother was likely unmarried and too young and too poor to look after a child – was just three days old when she first met Noreen. As Úna-Minh words it, they found each other in a city of 7.5million people.

"It's incredible," Úna-Minh says. "I was also not the first baby she saw. I think she had a few days of going around to orphanages and other places.

"The people at the hospital were incredibly supportive. They never asked for money; it wasn't like that. They just wanted to find a really good home for me."

Once the adoption process came together, a six-week-old Úna-Minh, previously destined for a Vietnamese orphanage, was heading instead for St Brendan's Park. She went on to attend primary and secondary school in Tralee before spending four years as a student of Irish and Journalism at Dublin City University (DCU).

Though she speaks fondly of Dublin, where she lived for 10 years, previously rare encounters with racism became more frequent upon moving to the capital.

"Maybe it's a population thing, or maybe it's because my mom and granda were so respected in Tralee, but I noticed it a lot more when I moved," she says.

"I was taken aback because of the perceived diversity of Dublin, the perception that we're always happy to say 'Céad Míle Fáilte', but there's so much racism and unseen racism that people experience on the streets or in certain parts of the city.

"It's sad because we [Irish people] have emigrated to so many countries and experienced discrimination abroad. I don't get why some of us are racist; it makes no sense.

"I find, due to today's politics worldwide, it's much 'easier' to be a racist nowadays. It's 'okay' because you'll get away with it; nobody will challenge you. A lot of times, people will fall back on 'freedom of speech' – but that doesn't equal freedom to hate.

"It's depressing. And because it's happened to me so many times, it's so boring. That may seem a strange word to use, but we go through this over and over, and it just becomes commonplace."

Úna-Minh today lives in Dundalk with her partner, Pádhraic, and is a freelance journalist who has worked for, amongst others, TG4 and trade union Fórsa. Since joining Twitter a decade ago, she has built a robust online profile and has used this status to promote the Irish language – a passion of hers and another result of her Irish-speaking grandfather's influence – in accessible, contemporary ways.

Her #frásaanlae (phrase of the day) efforts have helped win a following of over 12,000 Twitter users, and she regularly combines video-gaming with Gaeilge on the 'Twitch' streaming service.

Embracing the web, however, has left her more exposed to the world's losers, and 'Anseo' draws attention to some of the most outrageous racism she has sustained online.

"Initially, it used to make me angry, not upset," she says. "I feel like sometimes I've fought so long to be accepted as an Irish person – and then, especially online, I get told I can never be Irish. At this stage, I don't get dragged into arguing with these people. It can be upsetting, but I know I'm not going to change their mind; it's not my job to change their mind, and I have far more people who support me and don't care what these people are saying.

"At the same time, I do think it's important to highlight it because lots of people don't know it's happening. A lot of people say you're playing the 'race card' if you call it out and, also, they say 'If that happened to me, that's not how I'd deal with it'.

"Some online trolls get excited if you protect your tweets or take a break from Twitter; they see it as a victory. That leaves a tough balance because you don't want to give them that victory, but you also have to look after your mental health.

"The biggest thing I'd like people to take from 'Anseo' is that not all Irish people are white. We all have very different backgrounds. I'm 100-per-cent Irish, 100-per-cent

Kerry. That's why it was vital for me to launch the book in Tralee – around my friends, family, neighbours, and teachers."

The Kerryman, October 30, 2019.

Flying the rainbow flag in the Kingdom

Most celebrated when the marriage referendum passed in 2015, but how much did we know about the LGBT+ community, and have we given any thought to the struggles they continued to face after that historic vote? I hadn't; I suppose I fell into the trap of thinking that vote, huge and all as it was, solved all their problems. But, of course, it hadn't.

OVER five months in 2018 and '19, 138 people took part in research documenting LGBT+ life in Kerry. 'Visible in Kerry' – commissioned by Listowel Family Resource Centre in partnership with the HSE and KDYS – was launched last month and placed some tough reading before the public.

Many of the survey's young participants told of feeling unsafe at school and said they had suffered threats of physical assault because of their sexuality, gender identity, or both. While respondents reported feeling happier when they could be open about their identity, it remains common to feel uncertain, anxious, and even fearful of others' reactions.

Most adults surveyed reported positive experiences of being LGBT+ in Kerry, though many noted that rural life sets more challenges than urban life.

Tough reading – though not necessarily surprising reading.

"It was upsetting that my experience wasn't too dissimilar from the people in the research," says Dawn Linehan, one of five members of a new LGBT+ group, 'ScEEN In Kerry', present in the Ashe Hotel tonight. "I definitely identified with it, growing up here. I think we all felt that."

Perhaps the survey outlined what many felt they already knew, but that's different from saying the study was unnecessary. No matter how obvious, problems often roam free until we chalk down the data behind them; this was the first study of its kind conducted in Kerry and could yet trigger profound change in local LGBT+ life.

'ScEEN In Kerry' was a response to the survey, and member Karen Conway explains that the study has energised her colleagues, drawn the county's LGBT+ community together, and steeled them to address several issues the research underlined. The group's primary aims are to act as an online hub and provide more social outlets to Kerry's LGBT+ members countywide.

"The main theme of the survey is that people don't feel they have a place to meet people," says member Siobhán Johnston. "They don't feel visible. 'ScEEN In Kerry' is there to create events and spaces for people to come together.

"We've all come together through this, pretty much through word of mouth. We recently held an event here [at the Ashe Hotel], and there were around 50 people from all backgrounds there on the night – purely through Facebook promotion. That so many people came to the event without much of a push, publicity wise, was an achievement in itself.

"Now that we've established there's a need – from the research and the community in Kerry and Tralee – we're here to stay. Initially, the committee was to be just for the launch of the research but, because it's been so successful, we're staying together.

"Because Kerry is so wide and rural, we can't base ourselves in a physical building in one place – so we're like a virtual platform. That was a key recommendation in the research Niamh Bowen conducted. Listowel FRC and the HSE wanted us to be a virtual hub linking in with Listowel FRC's work."

Events to date have included movie nights and dance flash mobs. Owen Herlihy attended one of the latter having seen its promotion on Facebook, and tonight he's among the 'ScEEN In Kerry' members here to explain the group's work to *The Kerryman*.

The collective now wants to organise more social activities and events to encourage Kerry's LGBT+ community further. They say the absence of such outlets has pushed many people to move elsewhere to feel at home: to Limerick, to Cork, to Dublin, or further afield.

"People felt they had to move to a city," Siobhán says. "They had to move from their locality, literally, to find a community where they feel comfortable. That's not nice.

"I don't know if it's coincidental, but a lot more was going on here anyway; Madden's recently held a drag night, and a Kerry Pride event has been organised for the first time in years, in mid-June of next year. That needs to happen. I lived away for years, I came back to Kerry, I'd grown up here as a teenager, and when I first came back, it was like: 'Oh God, I'm the only gay in the village – this is terrible!'"

"In the last year and a half, though, we've all kinda ended up back here," Dawn says, "a lot of people have."

"Tralee is a different place now," Karen adds. "There's more going on; there's a movement happening.

"But that needs to be built on. We're taking action, we're motivated, we're building good structures, and we're excited for the future."

Another recent boost saw institutions such as Kerry County Council and Tralee Garda Station raise rainbow flags in response to 'Visible in Kerry'.

While the importance of such symbolic acts can be over-egged at times, ScEEN In Kerry welcomed the gesture. The 'Visible in Kerry' report underlined a lack of LGBT+ visibility, in workplaces especially, and seeing the rainbow flag fluttering so prominently in Kerry's capital was a step towards righting that.

It's four years since the same-sex marriage referendum, widely perceived as a seminal moment for Ireland's LGBT+ community – but while it confirmed a profound change to Irish legislation, it didn't and couldn't solve every issue the LGBT+ community faces. 'Visible in Kerry' proved that.

Robyn Fisher, for instance, points out that transgender people still face discrimination, intense bullying, and the highest suicide rate amongst the LGBT+ community.

What Owen feels the referendum has done, though – aside from legalising same-sex marriage – is open minds.

"I think when the marriage referendum passed in Kerry, a conversation started," he says. "A lot of people, especially in rural Kerry, mightn't have even talked about the LGBT community. For some people, the referendum was an introduction to something bigger, like what we're doing, which might have been more challenging before that. Nobody's trying to stop us, and everyone's dying to do something."

"We don't need to have or be at events all the time," Siobhán adds. "We can all do our own things. But it is nice to have the opportunity to attend events, whether you want to make friends, find a partner – or not feel as isolated as we might have before."

The Kerryman, November 13, 2019.

Reaching out to survivors of sexual violence

Vera O'Leary of the Kerry Rape and Sexual Abuse Centre in Tralee is one of the most informative and passionate interviewees I've met in the past four years. A 10-minute conversation with her contains more detail than you'll get in an hour with most others.

I don't know what it's like to have survived sexual violence, but I do believe that those who have can have faith in Vera to help them.

IT wasn't long after Vera O'Leary gave a recent radio interview when an elderly woman made a phone call to the Princes Quay-based Kerry Rape and Sexual Abuse Centre [KRSAC] and shared a decades-old burden.

Life had brought that caller much happiness since she'd survived being abused as a child – she had been married for some 50 years and had children – but she had never spoken to anyone of what she'd lived through.

Of those who contact the centre Vera directs, some present immediately after experiencing sexual violence.

Others, such as that caller, need years before they feel able to get in touch. Some never share their stories at all.

"There are people who suffer sexual violence but either can't name it for themselves, or their shame is so great that they couldn't imagine telling someone," Vera says today in the front room of the centre at Number Five Greenview Terrace. "They carry that with them, and the cost – perhaps in the form of abusing drugs or alcohol; relationships breaking down; failing school; mental health issues; or even suicide – is so high."

One hopes the establishment of a dedicated unit in Kerry for survivors of sexual violence, led by Inspector Paul Kennedy, will prove pivotal in reaching out to those shouldering such pain.

Its potential benefits are many: it will make it easier for victims to reach out to Gardaí, Vera feels, while the fact that the service even exists could see more survivors coming forward.

But one aspect in particular – that the two sergeants and 10 Gardaí who make up the unit have put themselves forward and have gone through an interview process and comprehensive training – gives Vera most hope.

"If a survivor comes forward and gets a compassionate, caring response to all their needs...It can be almost as healing as going through the criminal justice system, which is fraught with difficulties for those coming forward," she says. "We [KRSAC] have a great relationship with the guards. But a guard could come here, take a statement, and then have to follow up a burglary, anything. This unit is specifically tasked with sexual and domestic violence. Guards will build up expertise with the issue and the survivors.

"I feel there will also be a closer working relationship with KRSAC, which can only benefit survivors coming forward."

Though the CSO recently released data showing there were 23 reports of sexual offences in Kerry during the third quarter of 2018 – the highest third-quarter figure since 2010 – it's impossible, even for someone as knowledgeable as Vera, to articulate what precisely this figure says about society.

We do not know if these alleged attacks happened recently or years ago. There are also serious misgivings about the quality of Garda PULSE data, and the CSO issues the statistics 'under reservation'.

Considering that reported incidents only represent about 30 per cent of all sexual crimes committed, Vera explains, we also do not know how prevalent sexual violence truly is in Kerry today, and while the CSO has announced it will deliver a national survey on the issue, that process will likely take years.

"I do, however, know there is an increase in people coming forward," she says. "There are more people coming out after court with no issue being named or with talking to the media. That gives confidence to another person to say, 'I can talk. I can report it'.

"We also notice a lot more young people coming forward, but they're more reluctant to report…There's often the issue with young people that you could almost write a script: they're out but shouldn't be out; they're drinking when they're not supposed to be; they fancy the guy and, maybe, engage in some sexual activities. And then they're raped.

"For them, the difficulty is, 'Who is going to believe me?' We find it's often a parent that reports it, but then the young person is reluctant to make a signed statement."

While admitting some of the attitudes she has encountered recently – during discussions around the Belfast rape trial, to provide one example – still "horrify" her, she feels there has been a change for the better regarding modern views on sexual violence. That said, the issues society needs to tackle remain many and varied.

One such concern centres on the number of young people who do not understand what consent actually constitutes. Embedding a programme in the school curriculum is vital if this is to be addressed, Vera says, and while KRSAC currently delivers a pilot, its future is uncertain.

"We have a worker half a week, she goes to as many schools as possible, and NUI Galway is evaluating it," Vera says.

"It's funded externally, but when that funding runs out next year, unless I can raise funds through other means, we don't know if we can reach all the young people we need to reach.

"We have no problem being part of its development and don't mind being there as consultants. But it needs to be there, and teachers need to be trained up on it.

"I read a piece by a father recently: his son got into the car after school one evening and was really upset. The child said one of the kids wouldn't let him hug her good-bye. The father said, 'Sometimes, people don't want you to hug them – so you need to ask. If they say no, you need to say that's all right.

"I thought to myself, 'What a lesson he has given his son.'"

The Kerryman, January 23, 2019.

A chance encounter with absolute evil

The so-called 'Yorkshire Ripper', Peter Sutcliffe, murdered at least 13 women in Yorkshire and the north of England between 1975 and 1980. He also attempted to kill at least seven others.

One of those was Annie Rogulskyj (née Brosnan), who moved from Kilflynn to Yorkshire at a young age. She survived a savage attack by Sutcliffe in 1975 and would have likely died but for a neighbour startling the Ripper. After Sutcliffe died on November 13, 2020, Annie's brother, John, reflected on how a "lovely, bubbly" girl changed after that fateful July night in Keighley.

THE pain Peter Sutcliffe inflicted in the years leading up to his imprisonment in 1981 can't be measured just by looking at the number of lives he took and intended to take. 'The Yorkshire Ripper' murdered at least 13 women and attempted to kill at least seven others, but the impact of his brutality reverberated beyond his victims. His actions 40 years ago still cause hurt today.

Those he targeted were mothers, sisters, daughters, friends, and those who survived were not immune to the gravity of what they'd encountered.

Annie Rogulskyj was not the same person after Sutcliffe left her for dead in the early hours of Saturday, July 5, 1975, and her family hasn't forgotten what happened to her. When Sutcliffe died last Friday, Kilflynn's John Brosnan received a phone call from his daughter, who told him that the man who attempted to kill his sister 45 years ago had died. It's 12 years since Annie passed away, but she still matters, and what happened to her and her family in 1975 still matters too.

From Kilflynn to Keighley

"I've seen her called Anna in the news, but she was always Annie here at home," John told *The Kerryman* this week. "Our parents were Michael and Ellen, and Annie was one of 14 children. She was born in '33 and I was born in '34, so we were very close in age, and we were very close friends up until what happened. I suppose she just wasn't the same person after that; it had changed her – and why wouldn't it have?"

John and Annie grew up in Upper Tullig, Kilflynn, and John still lives there today. Annie, however, moved away at a young age, following their sister, Alice, to a West Yorkshire town. Some reports state she was 15 when she moved, but John believes she was more likely in her 20s.

In 1955, Annie married Roman Rogulskyj in her adopted town, Keyleigh, about 10 miles north-west of Bradford. She met Roman while she was working as a playing-cards sorter in Waddington's factory, and she became a well-liked figure in Keyleigh, earning the nickname 'Irish Annie' as she charmed locals with precisely the kind of bubbliness and loveliness that John had noted her for during their childhood: "I'm not surprised to hear she was popular. I couldn't see how she'd be anything but popular."

A chance encounter with evil

Annie and Roman's marriage broke down almost 20 years later; they divorced in 1973. Thereafter, she met Geoffrey Hughes, a man with whom she had a torrid relationship, according to Carol Ann Lee's acclaimed 2019 book, 'Somebody's Mother, Somebody's Daughter'. On July 4, 1975, an argument with Hughes led to an unplanned night out and a chance encounter with a man who would ruin and almost end her life.

A distraught Annie had, apparently, intended to visit her sister, but she wasn't in when she arrived at her home. She decided instead to have a couple of drinks at the Victoria Hotel and then caught a bus to Bradford, where she visited a West Indian nightclub. Friends accompanying her gave her a lift back to Keyleigh after the night out.

She returned home to discover that Hughes had moved out. There was no sign either of her kitten,

Dumdum, and she went back into the Yorkshire night towards North Queen Street and Hughes' house to confront him on the matter.

On her way, as she approached a local cinema, a man – Peter Sutcliffe – called out from a darkened doorway and asked her if she "fancied it". "Not on your life," Annie fired back, but it wasn't enough to perturb a man who would send chills through the north of England in the months and years ahead.

After getting to Hughes' house and flinging her shoe through his window, Annie turned back. As she passed an alleyway, Sutcliffe emerged from the shadows and propositioned her again.

Hospital examinations, which showed bruising on Annie's hands and right forearm, suggested that the Kilflynn native struggled to evade Sutcliffe, but it wasn't enough. He knocked her unconscious with one literal hammer blow.

According to UK Government documents seen by *The Kerryman*, Annie sustained severe head injuries – these included three crescent-shaped lacerations to her skull – and Sutcliffe inflicted several superficial slash wounds to her body. He would have likely delivered further, fatal injuries had a neighbour, looking to see what was causing the commotion, not startled Sutcliffe by shouting from a nearby property. The neighbour got no answer but Sutcliffe fled and left Annie to die. The attack happened between 1am and 2am, and a passer-by found Annie at about 2.20am.

She was rushed to Airedale Hospital and later transferred for a 12-hour operation at Leeds General Infirmary. Though given the last rites, she did recover, if only physically. She remembered nothing of the attack, and UK Government documents state that police would not link the crime to the so-called 'Ripper' murders until 1978.

"Yes, that was me," Sutcliffe confessed to police following his arrest in 1981. "I intended to kill her but I was disturbed."

Annie attended Sutcliffe's trial at the Old Bailey in May of 1981. He received 20 life terms for the murders of 13 women and the attempted murders of seven women, Annie included, but like any sentence, it could not erase what had happened.

"It was a waste of time to keep him in jail, feed him, and look after him," says John. "He was an awful type of man, and I won't say what should have been done to him!

"We did keep an eye on the coverage of the trial, but I've forgotten a lot of it now. It was 45 years ago, and time changes everything. It was a miracle and marvellous that she survived – but it was so unfortunate that it happened to her at all.

"Anybody would be happy to hear he's gone, but when your own family were affected, you'd be even happier, of course. That was my reaction on Friday when my daughter rang and after I heard it [again] on the one o'clock news."

A different person

Annie changed after that night. While she had been a regular visitor home, John says, that fell by the wayside following the attack.

"She was not the same woman," he says. "I never went over to Yorkshire to see her, and I wouldn't be certain, but I don't think she ever came back to Ireland."

She struggled to go out in public at all, actually. With the £15,000 she received from the Criminal Injuries Compensation Board, she bought a home and fitted it with tight security measures, according to "Somebody's Mother, Somebody's Daughter." In a later interview, she even said she had left her name behind.

"I'm not Anna," she said. "I will never be Anna again. I'm Joanna now. Anna died that night, and I wish I had died with her. I wish I had not had that operation, that there had just been the blackness and then no more."

A *Kerryman* search of a UK directory found a Joanna P Rogulskyj had lived at an address in Keighley. Her commitment to leaving her past name behind was real.

"My life is ruined," she said. "So I've had £15,000 from the Criminal Compensation Board. So what? No amount of money can give me back my anonymity, can give me back my lost boyfriends. No money can remove the stigma of the Ripper."

According to Kerry County Council burial records, Annie died of cancer at Airedale Hospital on April 4, 2008, and The Keyleigh News archives show that her

Funeral took place at Oakworth Crematorium. Her brother, Georgie, since deceased, travelled to the UK to bring his sister home at last.

"God, I do remember it, of course," says John. "We had Mass at Irremore Church, and then she was interred at the new cemetery in Kilfeighney. She was buried at a family plot."

She is survived by many relatives, five of her siblings among them: John, Mossie, Philomena, and Kathleen – all living in Kerry – and Betty, a London resident. Her family remembers her as more than a woman attacked by a monster, and that's how they'd like others to think of her as well.

"She was a good-living woman," John says. "A lovely, bubbly person."

The Kerryman, November 18, 2020.
Independent.ie, November 18, 2020.

'This message is for everybody. We can't have another Holocaust'

I've often been asked: 'Who's the most famous person you've interviewed?' I don't know, but it should be Tomi Reichental, a Slovakia-born Holocaust survivor.

I'll never understand what he lived through in the 1940s, but I'm grateful that he did his best to help me understand.

TOMI Reichental lost a rural Slovakian childhood to a nightmare in which he played hide-and-seek among corpses. In November 1944, the nine-year-old was bundled onto a cattle cart and sent to Hell on earth.

He was one of some 90,000 Jews driven from Slovakia in the 1940s, and the Dublin resident stands today as a living reminder of one of history's titanic crimes. He survived imprisonment in the Bergen-Belsen concentration camp, where some 70,000 people perished under the Nazi regime.

Listowel's Garden of Europe is home to Ireland's only Holocaust memorial, and Tomi has visited the north Kerry town many times – but if his regard for this part of the world is strong, the respect Listowel's young and old have for him is stronger. After attending a screening of his new film in the Classic Cinema of late, schoolchildren and adults queued to meet the 82-year-old, and their fascinated questioning kept him for hours. But, given the gravity of his recollections, that's the least one could wish for him.

"I was a child; I had been free. Next minute, I'm in a cattle cart with 50, 60 people for seven days," he says. "There was no privacy, no room, and the stench was unbearable. We had a barrel in the middle of the carriage, and that was our toilet. The journey to the camp was the most horrific experience of my life.

"When we got to Bergen-Belsen, we found Hell on earth. These skeletons were walking around with shaved heads and striped uniforms. We couldn't tell if they were men or women. They were terribly sick; they walked very slowly. Sometimes, they would drop dead right in front of you."

Tomi and his family had earlier fled towards Bratislava from their rural home after his father, Arnold, was betrayed locally and forced onto a train bound for Auschwitz. Arnold sidestepped death by jumping free from his carriage, and went on to join a resistance movement.

Tomi; his brother, Miki; and their mother, Judith, were soon captured themselves, but they were also among the few to survive the 'cleansing.' The family would reunite and return to Slovakia – but 35 of their relatives had perished by the War's end.

"By January 1945, the Germans were retreating, bringing prisoners with them to Bergen-Belsen," Tomi says. "The population exploded; huts built for 150 inmates now had 600. There was no room, no food – and I was hungry all the time.

"Disease broke out, and the crematoria couldn't cope. Thousands of bodies were left rotting in the open air. As children, we played among the corpses. We got used of the stench.

"We'd expected liberation because we knew the Germans were retreating, but it took months. One day, we heard rumbling, and we ran out to see jeeps, lorries, tanks. There were shouts: 'This is the British army. You are being liberated'.

"We were happy, but there was no dancing or celebrations; we were too sick. We just stood there, smiling and waving. We didn't have the strength to clap. I was a skeleton…I could have survived another two weeks, a month, not much more. It was not an extermination camp, but 70,000 people died at Bergen-Belsen, 12,000 afterwards because they were too far gone."

It was only the end of the beginning; Tomi, like all Holocaust survivors, was condemned to remember. Some 15 years after liberation, his profession – engineering – brought him to Ireland, where he married Evanne. She died of cancer 14 years ago, knowing her husband survived the Holocaust – but she knew little else of his time in Bergen-Belsen. For 55 years, Tomi did not speak of it.

It's wondrous, then, to think he appeared at this year's Listowel Writers' Week in front of almost 1,000 people. Last week, he was in Listowel again for multiple screenings of the Gerry Gregg-directed documentary film 'Condemned to Remember' – and further plans to screen for Kerry and Limerick schools in the New Year are at an early stage. Since evading the silence his hellish memories forced upon him, Tomi has spoken to some 100,000 students, and north Kerry has been particularly fortunate in regularly hosting the recollections of one of the last living witnesses of a nightmare made real.

"My biography, 'Til the Tenth Generation', was screened in Listowel, Saint John's Theatre, on April 15, 2010, exactly 65 years after my liberation," he says, "and I've been back many times since.

"It was incredible to be in the community centre… in front of 950 students, not far from Ireland's only Holocaust memorial. Kerry people have great respect. I was in Listowel with Gerry for packed screenings last week: one in the evening for community and another in the afternoon for schools. We always do a Q&A session after, and we were kept until 11.30pm on the Monday night. They had more questions, but we told them we had to get sleep!

"In 'Condemned to Remember', I wanted to show that Europe learned nothing. When the Jews wanted to escape, nobody wanted them. Today, refugees are trying to escape rape, murder, but nobody wants them…it's happening again.

"I travel Europe in the film, and you see the 1939 ideologies popping up in Hungary, Poland, Austria, even in Germany. In my native Slovakia, 10 per cent of parliament is held by the far right. Today, people parade in the uniforms of the people who terrorised my family. We need to be careful another tragedy doesn't happen to somebody else.

"This film is for everyone because we cannot forget. In 10, 15 years, there will be no Holocaust survivors left. If a teacher tells children about the Holocaust, only some will listen. In Listowel, nobody was playing on their phone or talking during the film because I was there. They will never forget."

The Kerryman, December 27, 2017.

First anniversary of lock-down: how COVID defined Kerry's news year

The COVID-19 pandemic made for the strangest period of my career, but it was a lot stranger and more challenging for others.

And some days in Kerry were particularly painful for some.

March 12, 2020: the announcement.

TODAY is March 10, and if we could travel back 12 months to this date in 2020, we'd find a Kerry almost unchanged.

There was uncertainty, but it fell short of fear. Some of our friends and family were attending day one of the Cheltenham Festival, but our questioning of their wisdom hadn't yet turned to certain fury. Face-masks seemed alien, never mind the idea that they would soon become a staple of common manners. What was five kilometres from our homes wasn't a world away. We didn't know we were verging on what would become a long, resigned sigh of a year.

Taoiseach Leo Varadkar told us, from Washington DC, that he needed to speak to us about Coronavirus. He shut our schools, colleges, and childcare facilities. It was the day we began to move apart, and we remain apart.

We don't know how many cases or deaths stemmed from those who travelled from Kerry to the Cotswolds, but on March 18, four days after the Cheltenham Festival ended, NPHET released the first of the county-by-county breakdowns we've listened out for each day since. It didn't provide numbers for 18 counties with fewer than five cases, but Kerry was not among the 18. The virus was here – six people had it – and 'the Cheltenham crowd' faced our blame, rightly or wrongly.

However it entered the Kingdom, it's still hurting us.

Kerry has performed better than most in pushing back against COVID, by sacrificing much of what we'd always taken as given. But we've all suffered. Some lost loved ones and couldn't say goodbye. Others beat COVID, but it scarred their health. Regardless of whether or not it hit us directly, we're all now left to look back at a year of COVID and how a virus we knew little about 12 months ago has shaped our news year.

May 19, 2020: the apology

POLITICIANS rarely do 'sorry', and the higher you go, contrition only becomes more scarce.

But by May 19, the known facts about Cahersiveen and its direct-provision centre were too damning for even a Minister to avoid the word. Charlie Flanagan was sorry – for some things, at least.

By then, Cahersiveen had campaigned for over a month for the Skellig Star Direct Provision Centre's closure. Its 69 residents were calling for the same; the children and adults living across its 56 bedrooms wanted out. Some 25 residents, most if not all of whom had moved by then, had contracted COVID-19.

The hotel only opened in mid-March when, in response to the pandemic, almost 100 asylum seekers were moved there from their emergency accommodation centres. By May 7, a Thursday, up to 30 people marched silently in Cahersiveen, but their placards spelled unity with the Skellig Star residents.

Twelve days later, *The Kerryman* reporter Sinéad Kelleher heard that the Justice Minister had reserved a full page of this newspaper having penned an open letter to Kerry's people, particularly those of Cahersiveen.

"I was working from home that Tuesday, and we were quite close to deadline," Sinead says. "There was only one word for it: unbelievable."

The Minister was sorry for the controversy around the centre's opening. He acknowledged the upset, anger, and suspicion within the community, and he regretted the extent to which his Department's actions had fuelled those feelings.

"But he didn't apologise to the asylum seekers," Sinead says. "I saw it as him being sorry for what had gone on but, to me, it didn't show concern for the conditions. It seemed he was sorry that local people were upset about it.

"It was actually his successor, Helen McEntee, who announced in July that the centre would close, and the residents had taken action in the form of a hunger strike before that happened. Action didn't immediately follow the apology.

"Some of the apology referred to the Department not having time to consult with the community ahead of the opening, but this turned out not to be true. There was plenty of time to consult with the locals. Negotiations for a centre in Cahersiveen had occurred six months before asylum seekers arrived there.

"It remains one of the most serious stories I've ever covered when you think of what people were put through."

November 19, 2020: the court sitting

GERRY Kennedy heard from the six o'clock news that the HSE was taking charge of Oaklands Nursing Home in Listowel. His brother, Seán, had lived there for four years and died there on November 13, aged 77.

He was a victim of the deadliest COVID outbreak in Kerry during 2020. Nine Oaklands residents died after confirmation of the first case in October, and every single resident would contract COVID. Five days after Seán's burial, a HIQA representative told Listowel District

Court that an inspection on November 4 found a nursing home in chaos. COVID-infected residents mingled with residents who'd not yet tested positive. On that same date, Seán was confirmed as having COVID.

"A few days passed from the diagnosis, and there was concern for his oxygen-saturation levels," Gerry tells *The Kerryman*. "When he was diagnosed, he had no symptoms, and then he developed a cough. They were monitoring him from around the eighth, and he died in the early hours of the 13th."

The November 4 HIQA inspection was the seventh at Oaklands in 2020. As early as June, HIQA visited a home it judged as 'non-compliant' to infection-control regulations. Gerry and all who loved the nine deceased Oaklands residents were left to wonder why it took until November 19 to cancel the registration of the company owning Oaklands: Bolden (Nursing) Ltd.

"Hearing it on the news, that was like a slap on the side of the head," Gerry says. To his knowledge, none of the deceased's relatives were aware of what was to unfold on November 19, and that day's events should have happened long before that.

Like all who died at Oaklands, Seán had a story ever before COVID. He was a Dublin native and had watched many matches alongside Gerry, and some of those were against the county he would make home, at The Writings in Listowel.

More than that, he was a loved father, grandfather, and brother, and last winter's events remain as vivid today for all who loved him.

"How do you rationalise it? It just doesn't bear thinking about," Gerry says. "I'll remember that Funeral until the day I die. The weather at the cemetery that day was the worst I've ever encountered. A storm blew in just as we arrived to have him interred.

"It's as raw today. If anything, it's rawer. He wasn't just a statistic, another number. He is sadly missed by us all."

December 25, 2020: the strangest Christmas

THERE was discussion aplenty of a "meaningful Christmas" ahead of the festive period, but the virus wasn't going to rest in late December.

Mid Kerry was faster than most in copping that, and it had to be. COVID bit the county's centre hard before Christmas, and nobody felt the pain more keenly than the community at Scoil Mhuire National School, Killorglin.

Scoil Mhuire was far from being the sole affected school, but it was unique at the time in being told by HSE South to close after confirmation of 17 COVID cases amongst its nearly 400 pupils. Children had to restrict their movements until December 30. Glen Evans' son – Colm, a sixth-class pupil – was among the confirmed cases, and Glen said he learned of an outbreak at

Scoil Mhuire on a Friday evening. Colm received his test the day after and the dreaded result on Sunday.

Glen worried for his household, including his 87-year-old mother, as COVID backed his family "into a corner".

"It was frightening," he tells *The Kerryman*. "Priorities flew out the window. You went from worrying about Christmas to what, at the time, was life or death for some people...My 87-year-old mother could have been a victim; I could have been a victim, who's to say? My wife, my three sons, including Colm, could have been. It was frightening for the whole town. You didn't know where it was going to stop. Every day brought a different challenge."

Other household members would contract COVID, and the house wasn't virus-free until January. Glen says his family had a horrible Christmas, but he and wife Tina kept the positives on show for the household's good.

"One person could be just finishing up with it, and another person might be starting with it. That's how COVID has survived, and it's why it's so sinister. We had a horrible Christmas, but you try to keep that away from the kids," he says.

"We got through it, and my mother was vaccinated a few days ago. Looking back, I don't hold the school at any fault; they were working to the government guidelines in place. I feel the government itself, though, could afford to use a little more common sense...If there's a spike in an area with a national school, close that school, and open it again when the situation is sorted."

January 29, 2021: the darkness

EVERYTHING about Corca Dhuibhne buzzes in normal times: its language, music, terrain, and people all give it the look and feel of a place apart. And for a long time, it felt like a conquest too far even for COVID.

As the initial lock-down eased, Dingle's magnetism pulled harder than ever as thousands chose the town for their summer 'staycation'. Locals fretted as their streets filled, but a predicted spike in cases – inevitable, most felt – wouldn't come to pass until long after the tourists left.

The first silent 'Wren' in memory was a dispiriting piece of history made, but then came real darkness. Case numbers climbed in December as the virus finally hit the peninsula with something like full force.

It got into one of two modules at West Kerry Community Hospital, and 20 of the module's 23 residents, as well as several staff members, contracted the illness. Nine patients succumbed to it; seven passed away in the hospital, while two passed on after being transferred to UHK.

There was only so much anyone could do or say in answer to what couldn't be changed, but a community did try to shine what light they could. Some lit candles and placed them at their windowsills. The board at An Díseart decided to place lights around its grotto for the month of February.

Since the 1990s, An Díseart at the former Presentation Convent has offered West Kerry a free space to explore spirituality and cultural events, informed by the lives led by early Christians at a time when people lived closer to nature.

The building is closed right now, but its gardens are open and gave a reeling community a focal point to consider what had happened over the winter.

"We wanted to see how the Díseart could serve the people of the town," says board chairperson Joan Maguire. "How could we respond to this enormous situation?

"Some places had left their Christmas lights up, but our tree was already down. We got the lights, and Breda Enright and Joe Garvey suggested we place them at the grotto. It was they who did the work of getting these lights on."

As soon as it's allowed, the building will again host classes and provide space for artistic endeavour. Its chapel will open for prayer. Until then, its gardens are there for everyone, seven days a week. The lights, for now, glow each night; they will for as long as darkness stays.

"Hopefully, after St Patrick's Day, there'll be enough light to carry us forward."

The Kerryman, March 10, 2021.

Part Four

Human Achievement

From California to Florida on a bike

I'll never understand why Tomás Mac an t-Saoir decides, every few years, to cycle through entire countries and continents. I get that he does it for an excellent cause, but it all sounds like a nightmare to me! Mind you, he seems to love it, so that's where he and I differ.

He also provides decent copy as he's always a very descriptive and open interviewee!

In 2016, he cycled the width of America – as you do.

BEFORE he embarked on the 41st and final leg of his Southern Tier cycle on Sunday, Tomás Mac an t-Saoir sipped on a cup of coffee and indulged in a daydream.

Sitting and watching as a new morning introduced itself to Gainesville, Florida, the young cyclist thought ahead to arriving at America's east coast and dipping his toes in the Atlantic Ocean for the first time in six weeks. He looked ahead to Christmas and returning home to his family pub in west Kerry, but he used the bulk of those minutes to fish through the memories he'd gathered over the previous two months and 3,000 miles.

When the Ballyferriter native spoke to *The Kerryman* in October, his confidence was striking for a man facing a coast-to-coast slog across a nation the size of a continent. The 22-year-old cycled 7,000 kilometres in 2016 ahead of touring America's southern states and, having completed expeditions across vast portions of Spain, he was bullish ahead of his American assignment.

"I wasn't scared when I started out. I knew 3,000 miles was a big ask, but much of the Southern Tier route is flat, so I felt confident," Tomás said this week. "But I couldn't have prepared for everything the journey has thrown at me…When I crossed the border into Florida, I met a vicious headwind, and I covered just 27 kilometres in two hours. It was demoralising. Then a storm arrived, and I had to take shelter under a McDonald's canopy for seven hours.

"My predicament was worsened by the fact that no taxi driver would pick me up because I had a bike with me. Thankfully, a kind local got wind of my situation on Facebook and came down to give me a lift to a nearby hotel.

"That experience was nearly as bad as the Texan ghost town I was stranded in for six hours one Sunday…I'd cycled for hours and ended up in this shell of a place; nothing was open. Border patrol eventually had to come get me and bring me to Del Rio. I was lucky to get out of that one!"

He pedalled his way around all those obstacles, however, and on Sunday afternoon, he rolled into the coastal city of Saint Augustine, the 41st and final stop on his six-week schedule. He unfurled an Irish flag and posed for a celebratory Snapchat photo in front of the Atlantic before scampering off for a pint of Guinness and a chat with fascinated locals.

As he nursed his stout, his thoughts turned to those who'd pushed him along. Before leaving for America, Tomás stated that the late John Browne, a legend of Corca Dhuibhne cycling, would never leave his side. John dominated his apprentice's mind throughout the sprawling route. The people of Kerry have also travelled with Tomás via Twitter, Snapchat, Facebook, and other online platforms, and he acknowledged that their encouraging words kept the pedals twirling during hours blighted by loneliness, headwinds, and heat.

But it was the American people who ensured Tomás' access to the essentials in providing him with meals, advice, and accommodation throughout his quest – and he repaid their generosity by introducing them to Dónal Walsh's timeless #LiveLife message.

"I'll forever be grateful to the American people for following my journey and helping out at every pit stop, and I've been doubly delighted at their reactions to Dónal's story," he said. "I've scattered the #LiveLife message all along the Southern Tier, and the American people have shared their experiences of depression and suicide with remarkable honesty. It's a big problem in the US, too…I think #LiveLife left its mark on them. They've been most generous in donating to the cause over these last 3,000 miles."

Tomás' focus has since drifted from reminiscence to times ahead. Though he only returned to Ireland this week, bringing with him admittance that the cycle has drained both his physical and emotional resources, he's already scribbling down plans for the coming months.

He'll relax over Christmas by catching up with his family, friends, and girlfriend, and he'll juggle his downtime with work in the family pub and a few cycles over the local Slea Head drive, where his now-frothing passion for the sport first simmered. But one American venture hasn't satisfied Tomás' hunger for touring.

"When I was in Pensacola in Florida, I got talking to someone about a cycle tour in Scandinavia next summer," he shared. "We'll have to discuss it in more depth, but I hope to do another cycle next year in aid of #LiveLife again. Until then, I'll work and cycle. I'm back to my old routine!"

The Kerryman, December 14, 2016.

Why do it at all?

Two years later, Tomás was 'at it' again. This time, he was preparing to cycle the length of Africa.

As you can tell from my intro to the previous piece, I still haven't answered the title I put on this article, but it's always interesting to try and get some sense of why Tomás pushes himself so much.

THERE are hard-earned pints of Guinness – and then there's the pint Tomás Mac an tSaoir nursed in Gainesville, Florida, two winters ago.

It brought an end to a 7000-kilometre cycle spanning two months, the width of the United States, and more moments of note than some experience in a lifetime. But by the time he got in touch with *The Kerryman* hours later, a thirst for greater things than Guinness was already forming.

Not even two years on, he's enjoying a rare date with relaxation in Green Street's 'Bean in Dingle' café and sipping on a cappuccino whilst thinking ahead to this Friday – the day he'll fly to Cairo, via Istanbul, to take on a solo cycle with no definite end date.

"All I know is that I'll finish in Cape Town, hopefully around St Patrick's Day," he says. "That'd be class. But it could be April, May – I don't know, really."

If that sounds flippant, it's at odds with his perspective on the challenge.

All going well, next spring, he'll conquer a route that's roughly twice as long as the one he overcame in the States, and he'll have added 12 African nations to an already spectacular cycling résumé.

Up until two days ago, it would have been true to say the primary emotion he felt was excitement. Since then, there have been tearful goodbyes and shreds of anxiety. The length of the journey is one thing; that he'll cycle alone through some of the most dangerous nations on earth, another entirely.

"Around 80, 85 per cent of people are against this," he says as he leans against the adjacent windowsill. "But people say countries are dangerous – but it's really that there are dangerous regions in those countries. The route I've planned is probably the safest you could plan in the circumstances.

"For example, Sudan has probably got the worst reputation of any of the countries on my list – but the way it's planned, it'll probably end up being the safest country I'll travel through. Apparently, they're among the most welcoming, hospitable people you'll meet, where I'm travelling through, and I'm looking forward to that.

"The country I'm most worried about is Ethiopia because I've heard kids will throw stones and run at cyclists all day long; it's like their national sport. But, look, there are parts of towns and cities in Ireland you wouldn't be advised to cycle through...aren't there?

"There's a place on the border between Ethiopia and Kenya where there's been open conflict recently and, yeah, I'm worried about that, of course I am. But I've been in touch regularly with the Department of Foreign Affairs, and they've me up to speed on keeping in touch with them throughout so they can let me know of any no-go areas, where to stay, that kind of thing – and I'll be meeting them along the way, too."

Physically, he feels as tuned up as ever, helped in part by a difficult recent cycle from Belfast to Kerry. The thought of toiling in the infamous African heat is similarly low on the 24-year-old's hefty list of concerns; while in the States, he became well-acquainted with 40-degree days.

But with the majority of friends and family holding at least some reservations about what Tomás will attempt alone, why he's even allowed himself to indulge the thought of an African tour is a question in itself.

It's curious to listen to someone express a deep love of Corca Dhuibhne one minute before turning around and saying a continent he's never visited is "in his blood".

It was an old friend who put the idea to Tomás first day – and it would seem the very things that would put most of us running from such a challenge were what enticed the Baile an Fheirtéaraigh man into a much closer look.

"It's easily the most difficult continent to cycle, the top tier, the holy grail of cycling tours," he says.

"But once I pulled out a world map, it was as if Africa came out, punched me in the face, and said, 'Have you got the balls to cycle me?' I'm stubborn, I'm determined, and once the idea was in my head, I was glued.

"I googled it, and people had close calls – but they got through it, and they loved it. As for doing it alone, at least if something happens me, it only happens to me. Whereas if there were another person – would I want that on my conscience later?"

But the greatest influence of all on his decision to leave Ireland; his family; and his girlfriend, Éadaoin, for up to seven months was not the challenge, the continent he describes as his holy grail.

As was the case two years ago, he'll raise funds for the late Donal Walsh's #LiveLife charity and spread its message beyond this island – and past experiences of bringing #LiveLife to new places have steeled his conviction.

"Like so many people, I heard Donal speaking on 'The Saturday Night Show' with Brendan O'Connor. He was only 16 at the time, suffering with cancer, and I remember thinking he spoke like he was 60 or 70," Tomás says. "I think suicide and mental health are kind of taboo subjects in this country, but it's getting better. And

I wanted to bring that message elsewhere because it's a problem everywhere; that's what this is about. If I can inspire one person in Africa, it'll be worth it.

"I remember when I was in Louisiana two years, it was illegal to cycle across the Mississippi Bridge, and a truck driver picked me up. When I told him what I was cycling for, he opened up about the breakdown of his marriage and the difficulty he was having seeing his children. He was contemplating taking his own life.

"We exchanged contact details, and he got back to me a time later to tell me he'd sorted out his issues and was in a much better place, and he referred back to the conversation we'd had.

"That's what it's all about; that's the whole thing. That was one chat in a seven-week trip – and it was enough to make it worthwhile."

The Kerryman, October 24, 2018.

Footnote: Tomás completed his journey in Cape Town the following May.

No pain, no gain, no lifelong memories

Dingle man Shane Finn has taken on several extraordinary challenges on behalf of a charity and a cousin close to his heart. The biggest of all was in 2019.

HE finished 12 marathons in 12 days in 2014, and 24 in 24 days in 2017.

So for those who didn't read deeply into Shane Finn's recent crossing of America, stepping up to a 36-day challenge may have seemed like logical progression. Or at least as logical as things go in the world of Finn.

But when one breaks down the numbers, the Dingle man's newest set of accomplishments is as comparable to 2017's 24-day challenge as K2 is to Carrauntoohil.

Back then, it was all running. This time, he was on his bike twice as often as he was on foot, and by day 19, he'd cycled the equivalent of scaling Everest twice, with 97,000 calories left for dead. He returned from the States eight and a half pounds lighter than he was upon leaving Ireland.

He swapped the four-to-five-hour days of '14 and '17 for 7am-to-9pm shifts, and when one takes account of altitudes of up to 11,000ft, and a climate as changeable as an adolescent's temperament, you have yourself a confrontation against all that's unnatural.

"I felt fatigued from around day 23 or 24," he says. "It was hard to catch up with the tiredness. Good sleep and good food wasn't enough. I was scraping the bottom of the barrel, trying to stay safe on the road.

"The plan was to do rotations of three days running, three days cycling. That changed to four days cycling and two days running to make up ground after getting snowed in for a day in the Rockies. We couldn't even move our camper vans that day. We only got back on track on the third-last day.

"I was playing catch-up the whole way. I knew all along I was going to make it, but the pressure was on. If we'd been snowed in another day, we were in major trouble.

"It [the weather] used to change instantaneously, with the click of your fingers. On my descents, I'd be frozen solid at the bottom of the hill. My water bottles would be frozen solid.

"There were all sorts of problems, tornado warnings in Kansas, everything – but we got it done."

If his words read as cocky, like those of a man trying his hardest to sell achievements that don't need much promotion as it is, his tone is at odds with all that; every utterance is natural and matter-of-fact.

Many questioned whether or not his American Ultra was a wise undertaking to begin with, and those doubts will long outlive his American toil. But Shane was, possibly, as prepared as one can be for such extraordinary circumstances.

In his own words, he was a freak about his food and his training for six months. Becoming as fit as possible was, naturally, among his goals beforehand, but even that was secondary to steering clear of injuries.

"During training, if I felt I was getting tired or run down, I'd take a day off," he says. "It was very important to listen to my body.

"It's a skill that's taken me four years to master, and it's a hard thing for me to do because I'm an energetic person. But I know now that if I take a break, I'll be able to recover.

"I worked closely with my GP beforehand, got bloods done, ECGs. I was working with a sports-science team in Dublin testing my lungs, my internal organs, doing VO2 max texting, blood-lactate testing, heart-rate testing. Everything came up clear, and I got my thumbs up.

"A typical weekend involved a gym session on Friday nights, and I'd be out on the bike on Slea Head again in the morning. On Saturday, I'd do another couple of hours on the bike and another gym session that night.

"On Sunday mornings, I used to run a marathon before Mass. I'd get home after Mass, eat, and then, maybe, go for another run or cycle. When I flew into America first, in February, I stayed at altitude. It took its toll being there so long and pushing myself so hard. I could feel myself losing a bit of power in the legs."

Since returning home, the aches accumulated over the past year have been ebbing away, slowly moving aside to allow for gentler exercise.

They've been overpowered, as well, by feelings of gratitude for the team that accompanied him: namely his father, Timmy; physio Allie McCann; a three-man film crew; local man Anthony McGovern; and Martin Fahey of Spina Bifida Hydrocephalus Ireland [SBHI], the charity Shane raised awareness and funds for.

And his memories of finishing in New York, of being greeted by his family and his first-cousin, Mary Evans, the inspiration fuelling his support of SBHI, soothed the agony still further.

"The smile on her face wiped a lot of the pain away," he says.

"€250,000 [the initial fund-raising target when he set off] was a lofty goal. I'd say we won't be too far off €100,000. The dynamic was very different given that I was away from my own country. Considering everything, though, we still did pretty well.

"At the moment, I'm back home and doing a bit of teaching with Sacred Heart University and speaking at various events.

"I'm doing my best now to just enjoy my training because everything has been so calculated for about a year.

Every beat, every heart rate, every session, I was keeping notes about how I felt. Mentally, that's draining as well.

"I won't be doing a 48-day challenge for a long, long time, and I'll take a break from ultra-endurance…I can't take the piss. I have to respect my body – because it has served me well so far."

The Kerryman, June 12, 2019.

Swimming where no one dares

Dingle swimmer Nuala Moore puts her body and mind to the sternest test when she hits the ocean. I spoke to her after she swam 1.7 kilometres at 59 degrees south – in a sea in which 10,000 people have died.

NUALA Moore says she's 100-per-cent normal – "always will be" – and in sitting behind the counter at the homely Strawberry Beds bedding shop on Dingle's Green Street, she couldn't be further removed from what she calls her "streaks of greatness".

The latest such streak saw her swim 1.7 kilometres off the Americas' southernmost point, Cape Horn, in water termed 'the graveyard of ships', a sea that has claimed some 10,000 lives. A maritime saying summarises the enormity of her feat: "Below 40 degrees south, there is no law; below 50 degrees south, there is no God." Nuala swam at 59 degrees.

Listening to her today, it feels as though she's mastering a life that tackles extremity between vast periods of normality. But this, she admits, is a contradiction that previously caused her discomfort.

Her list of swims includes locations such as Switzerland, Russia, the US, China, Estonia, Finland, Germany, and Argentina. Before all that was a six-person round-Ireland relay and an intensely physical and emotional journey over two months in 2006.

Her accolades include being twice listed as one of open-water swimming's 50 most adventurous women, and in her mind she can still hear the waves from her recently ratified swim of the maritime boundary between the Pacific and Atlantic. Returning from that to everyday life, however, has been no small challenge in itself.

"When you finish an event like the round-Ireland – it took everything from me physically, financially, emotionally – and then walk in here [her shop], and you've to reconcile the two things," she says. "When you swim off Cape Horn, you're a superhero; you turn the key in that door, and you're a normal person.

"Sometimes you want to scream from the rooftops: 'Do you know how phenomenal I am?'…but the world has moved on. It took me the bones of a year and a half to learn how to reconcile that."

By her own admission, she loves to face a curveball, and the waves south of the Americas could have wrecked her ambitions at any time.

But to describe her as someone with no regard for safety would be a gross inaccuracy. Alongside her many battles against the extraordinary, she lists Coast Guard involvement; work with Ocean Extreme Medicine;

decades of first-aid, CPR, and defibrillator teaching; and 24 years of PADI diving up to professional level amongst her safety credentials.

She has travelled the world to present on scientific, acclimatisation, rescue, and medical aspects of ice swimming. Of late, she has worked with Dr Patrick Buck on safety for all water users; she speaks today of the need to tackle drowning issues and reduce the number of people requiring mountain-rescue assistance.

Her recent challenge leant on the support of safety rescue divers Catherine Buckland and Chris Brooker – both of whom work in the Antarctic – and detailed extraction and remote emergency-care plans were in place.

For all that experience, when it came to hitting the sea, she broke into tears and repeatedly asked how her team planned to get her out; there was no land visible east or west, and her accompanying boat would be some 200 metres away.

"I'm faced with the reality that my crew is saying 'we are 24 hours from emergency care'. I looked at the challenges and the variables. What I didn't look at is the strain it would add to my breathing, anxiety, and stress levels," she says.

"When you put a team in place, their job is to watch you and spot potential dangers. Catherine and Chris get people from water at speed. They watched me throughout, but it's really hard to spot a little hand. That scared me.

"One would be a spotter; one would get to me. I need to stay calm above the waves. I had straps around my waist, so they're not grabbing at just togs if they need to get me. There were straps at the side of the zodiac [the vessel used] to secure me.

"Over the years, you build up a team that knows how you respond when things hit the deck and knows how to handle you, which is important. They need to be there for you, they need to push you as far as is safe, but they also need to know how far you can push yourself."

Planning, obviously, changes to suit the scale of the event at hand – but Nuala insists on proper preparation regardless of the challenge one is squaring up to.

As a society, she feels we've lost touch with our survival instincts. Work, family, finances, and more have compromised our ability to oversee our safety. In addition, our tendency to work as groups has narrowed our capacity to work alone should a difficult situation arise.

"I met a guy hitching about two months ago, and he was heading up Mount Brandon. I stopped and said, 'It's a really bad day,' and he said, 'But it's the only day I have'. That's not the point. People are pushing themselves too hard to do these things between all of the stresses taking up their time," she says.

"A lot of people are inclined to work in groups, but when an event happens, and you're on your own, you need skills to operate on your own. In my opinion, not everyone is preparing for a negative outcome. We have to have a safety plan."

She will continue in her efforts to boost our knowledge of safety from here. She plans on becoming the first person to traverse the waters between Kells and Dingle since the 1960s, and she hopes to swim around the Great Blasket.

"For now, though, I'm going to try and get this head down," she says. "It's way up there since Cape Horn."

The Kerryman, April 18, 2018.

Part Five

Hard to Define

'Where a goat is King, and the people act the goat.'

I'd never been to Puck Fair before visiting in 2017. I went there with photographer Michelle Cooper-Galvin, who thankfully knew her way around Ireland's craziest festival – because I was like a lost child.

THE Laune's current is too soft to drill into one's attention on a regular afternoon – but its gentleness is the very thing that marks it out from the frenzy of Puck time.

Once you cross the Laune Bridge on August 10, you enter a world of the stuff usually reserved for the most vivid dreams. For three days, the small town of Killorglin restyles itself as something resembling a Turkish market-place, a thicket of stalls bidding for the attention of the hyperactive thousands.

An obviously experienced fair-goer rips through sheets of people on Lower Bridge Street, a roll of fluffy beige carpet resting on his young shoulder. Most of the fair's patrons hike in the opposite direction, against the sloping street, as if marching to the hectic notes of piano accordion jetting from the town's megaphones. Their aim: to secure a decent vantage point for the annual fair parade and the crowning of a wild mountain goat as their King. Try explaining that one to an outsider.

"It's been 55 years since we first made off Puck," says Michael Buckley from Moyvane, waiting for the parade from behind a steel barrier with his brother, John. Both men sport suit jackets as smooth as black pebbles for their big day out.

"Once ever I missed it – I'd been sick – but other than that, myself and the brother have made it off every whole year. John has never missed a Puck Fair – and it's always the crowning of the goat we get the most kick out of."

The fair is the clearest expression of Kerry's inherently quirky spirit, and it's our weakness for the bizarre that has marked Puck as unmissable for the Buckleys and many like them. A few paces away from the Moyvane brothers, Patricia O'Sullivan from Cromane Lower is celebrating her 40th Puck, in the company of her grandchildren – Liam and Jack McGrath – and the boys' mother, Ciara. Every year, the ways of Puck are passed on as well as celebrated, and Patricia and company are a case in that point.

At the top of the Square and the opposite end of the experience spectrum, Colette Calder introduces her little boy, Cameron, to his first Puck, the weird concoction that has made his town famous.

His eyes beam as the parade slithers to the toes of the Square, and he looks up at his Mom as stewards help the white-caped 2017 Queen of Puck, 12-year-old Caitlin Horgan, from the penultimate float.

Thousands of cheers as sharp and clear as glass pour over the barriers as the last float snails to the most anticipated of halts. Four guards approach the float and hoist a pen holding Rí na gCnoc, the King of Puck, to the base of a massive platform at the top of the town. There, young Caitlin is waiting with a silver Brian de Staic crown worthy of this king, the world's most revered mountain goat.

A chunky hook lifts the goat's pen to its perch and the apex of 400 years of history, and Seán Ó Sé powers into his familiar rendition of 'An Poc ar Buile'. Ireland's strangest fair is underway – and, with that, it completes yet another lap of the calendar.

"Welcome to Killorglin," emcee Declan Mangan cheers, "where a goat is King, and the people act the goat!"

The Kerryman, August 16, 2017.

Recapturing fond memories to a Heavenly Kingdom backdrop

If I remember correctly, my Editor, Kevin Hughes, met New York firefighter Tim Grant in Killarney a few days before this interview took place. He got a number for Tim, who apparently had a great story to tell. It was an unusual one, but it was certainly worth meeting him in Dingle as he talked me through an eventful-but-wonderful few days in the Kingdom.

IT was a chain of coincidences and charmed turns so improbable that it caused a New York Fire Department member to describe it as 'Heavenly'. Fireman Tim Grant says he's experienced "a million stories" in Kerry – but none are as beautiful as the one he's recounting by the stove in O'Flaherty's Bar, Dingle, this night.

As the Long Island resident dug through photos in looking ahead to his umpteenth visit to Kerry, he happened upon a picture from a Kingdom adventure of old – one his eyes had scarcely encountered in the 23 years since passed. In it, two 'brothers' of his – 'Bronko' Durell Pearsall, who died on 9/11, and the recently deceased Joe Murphy – were looking out at him. Tim took it as a sign they were saying hello from Heaven, and he took to Facebook that day to say as much.

He knew the picture was taken on the Ring of Kerry; he was less certain of its exact location. But its reappearance prompted a wish to revisit 'Heaven', some stony hillside overlooking what, he felt, might be an inlet sourced from Dingle Bay.

"I'm a New York city fireman, been on the job 25 years," he says. "I'm also in the FDNY Emerald Society bagpipe band, and we do a lot of travelling together. A couple of trips I made to Ireland were with those guys. Five of us came over here in 1995 and rented a van and travelled all over.

"At the time, we went to Killarney, but it was so long ago. I remember we did part of the Ring of Kerry, and I thought we did it counter-clockwise because there was water on our right as we came from the town.

"I have tons of pictures of that trip, and this one was of my buddy, Bronko. Also in the picture was Joe Murphy, who passed away two years ago…It's almost as if they called me to say 'hi' and knew I was going to Ireland in a week's time.

"I said to my daughter, Jessica, that I wanted to set out on a mission and try and find that exact spot – and we did that."

As his friend, Tim Murphy; daughter Jessica; and her girlfriend, Maggie, hit the 'Ring' on a mid-morning last week, taking the anti-clockwise route Tim's faded memories recommended, the four-strong collective gained energy from its first sighting of Dingle Bay – but, in the ensuing hours, the search stumbled from one false dawn to another.

Their car eventually rolled into Kenmare, by which time Tim's dreams had lost their colour. He knew he'd missed his target, but his hopes reignited with a fortunate misstep.

"I'd given up on it," he says. "We had lunch, but then we made a wrong turn from the Ring on the way back to Killarney. We took this side road to get back to the Ring, and it took us towards the national park; we saw water. We decided to take a left instead of turning back towards the Ring – and there were the lakes. I said to my friend, Tim, 'All I could remember was a zig-zaggy road – and this is a zig-zaggy road'.

"This whole trip it's been pouring, and out of nowhere, this bright light came out. 'They're leading you to this spot; they want you to find it,' Tim said to me. And, sure enough, I started to remember. We came up to Ladies' View, and we found the exact spot from the picture."

Posing with Jessica – who was just one year old on 9/11 but has grown up to stories of 'Bronko' – Tim took to video and recreated a moment of such power it shook him to tears.

"It was a special moment," he says with a shake of the head. "We're a very, very tight group [the New York Fire Department].

"Bronko was like a brother. On September 11, I was told at around 10pm that night that he'd been working, and I knew then that he was gone. Joe died two years ago; he had some health problems.

"We were here for four nights in Killarney for the Irish dancing championships with Jessica and Maggie. We're spending two nights in Dingle, and we're going on to Ennis now. I love Kerry, and I've got a million stories…but for the sun to come out like that and bring us to the exact spot where we took that photo in 1995 – I can only describe it as Heavenly."

The Kerryman, February 21, 2018.

From Dublin to Kells to Chelsea

I'd spoken a couple of times to Billy Alexander about the unusual gardens he keeps in Kells, south Kerry, before doing so again in 2018. The plants that make up his Kells Bay House and Gardens facility are not what you'd expect from that part of the world. But that's what makes them prize winners.

FOR those in Billy Alexander's line of work, exhibiting at the Chelsea Flower Show is the pinnacle.

But reaching the top in one's field often brings its own difficulties. For those who reach the summit, the only way from there, you'd think, is down.

Owner of the 44-acre Kells Bay House and Gardens – home to plants more associated with the southern hemisphere than south Kerry – Billy doesn't play down the prestigious show; it is, he says, "the Olympics" of his profession.

But for those who know the Dublin man and love his Kells masterpiece, it's reassuring to hear his mind has already turned to the future – a future in which his south Kerry gardens will continue to flourish.

"It's a special place," he says. "I've given up everything for Kells Bay. Now, I want to promote the place to the world."

Before a climber conquers a mountain, they start from a base. Yesterday, Billy reached gardening's summit as the first visitors streamed into Chelsea's Great Pavilion, an expanse that could pass for an indoor Garden of Eden.

With a Silver Gilt accreditation and a chat with Queen Elizabeth II, he had completed his transformation from a Dublin gardener to a world-renowned figure in his field by day's end.

"The queen showed great interest in the ferns," he said. "She was curious as to where it came from, and I told her it came from Kells Bay, Kerry, where her grandmother, Queen Victoria, once visited.

"We were truly honoured to be chosen to exhibit at Chelsea this year, and winning the Silver Gilt medal was the icing on the cake."

His gardening journey began 20 years ago and led to this exhibit, a sample of Kells' offerings for the eyes of expert judges and gardening enthusiasts, royal or otherwise.

"One thing led to another," he says of his early years in horticulture. "I got other plants and tree ferns, and the Vogels, the previous owners of Kells Bay, invited me down. They wanted to buy some of my ferns.

"I went to Kells in 2000 for the first time. A couple of years later, I was looking for a new garden in southwest

Ireland because my Leopardstown garden was chock-a-block. That's when I was drawn to Kells, which I described at the time as a beautiful wilderness. I bought it in 2006."

In committing to what he today calls his "passion-fuelled business", he moved with his wife, Penn, to south Kerry in 2012 to tend to a site as rich in history as it is in greenery.

Much of Billy's knowledge of the site's Victorian house comes from what's anecdotal as opposed to what's written, but he fills in the gaps as best he can: built in 1838 as a dormer bungalow, it served as a hunting lodge for the Blennerhassets.

Since acquiring the site, Billy has overseen projects that produced infrastructural fruits such as a renovated driveway, water features, a Thai restaurant, and new walks through all of the garden's main arteries.

The gardens are home, also, to the 112-foot 'skywalk', Ireland's longest rope bridge – but the site's 'exotica' plants, species you'd sooner expect in Australia, New Zealand, South America, and Indochina, remain his business's heartbeat.

"A lot of things make it possible for these plants to flourish," he says. "We're in a v-shaped valley, protecting us from the worst of the winds. There's acid-rich soil; rain that comes in from the Atlantic free of pollution; and the Gulf Stream, which affords us milder winters.

"I practice what they call Robinsonian methods. If I saw a nice primrose in your garden, I'd get the seeds, scatter them, and let them grow in profusion. I let the plant do the talking."

His heart and attention will remain with Kells in the long term – but his immediate focus is on London's East Road.

Since first competing in Bloom over a decade ago, Billy has never left Ireland's equivalent of Chelsea without some form of recognition and, last year, he won "Best in Show", the breakthrough that made Chelsea participation possible.

"I met with some Welsh friends, who are big into plants, at a seminar two years ago, and they said, 'Billy, you should do Chelsea!" he explains. "I'd never even thought of it because it's like saying, 'you should go to the Olympics even though you haven't been training.' But when I was named 'Best in Show', I decided to go for it.

"You've to tell the organisers why you're doing it, what you're bringing, where it's coming from, and how organic and sustainable it is. What we're doing in Kells ticks a lot of those boxes.

"In September, they got back to me and gave me what was, effectively, an invitation. Then I started thinking, 'Oh my God, what have I done?' It was surreal."

Like many climbs, the closing stages were the toughest. Apprehensive rather than nervous, he began his work on 'Wilde Atlantic Garden' in the pavilion last week, and the pressure Billy felt ahead of yesterday's opening day must have been the severest he has ever dealt with.

"With Chelsea, there's a lot of paperwork between corporate passes…guest tickets; it goes on and on," he says. "Even when my lorry arrived, it had to be booked in; if you miss your slot – you're in big trouble. It's been hugely time-consuming. The Saturday before last, for example, was sort of an off day; I got a haircut because I didn't have the chance before that!"

But the exhibit's contents and name are, in part, reminders of what the toil has been about.

Staycity has covered his transport and expenses, and while in London, Billy will stay in the company's 'Wilde' aparthotel. The exhibit's name is a tribute to their generosity – but it's also a nod to the Wild Atlantic Way. The stand itself features ferns, moss, and rocks from Kells – a place that has no less of a hold on Billy now than when he first encountered it 18 years ago.

"This is about promoting Kells as a destination; that's the main reason behind this."

The Kerryman, May 23, 2018.

Broadway lights in sight for the Kingdom's Fred Astaire

Even though he's a Dingle man, I don't think I'd ever spoken in person to former World Irish Dancing Champion David Geaney before this 2018 interview. He's an ambitious fella, and even winning World Championships wasn't enough to stop him aiming higher – if it's possible to aim higher. Bringing a show to Broadway, though, was kind of a big deal.

THE fine weather brings out the best in everything. It's been a summer of sunshine thus far but, this week, there was heat to match.

When such weather hits Dingle, a city-like buzz pulses through a town of only 2,000 people. Here and there, tourists sit out with their teas and coffees, revel in the midday sun, and tap along to the trad music flowing from shops and bars. The odd pint of cider makes an appearance, too – but who's to judge on days like these?

It's the kind of atmosphere five-time Irish Dancing World Champion David Geaney feeds off. When night falls, those tourists are drawn to his steps and the rattle his metal-tapped dancing shoes drum up on the Dingle Pub's timber platform. While perched on a stool overlooking his bar's dining area today, he speaks fondly of his championship-winning days; as he puts it himself, "I'd go into battle for a bag of chips." But even for a man of his competitiveness, facing a crowd, jamming to a musician, and applying an artistic touch to his craft has an allure above any other.

"When I got to 16, I kind of got sick of competition rules and wanted to venture into performance and choreographing my own stuff," he says. "In competition, I was coming up with things people weren't doing and tweaking things other people were trying. I forgot about judges; it was about performing to an audience.

"I was about 19 when I was coming to the end of my competition days and, by then, I always freestyled if I felt it was going to come right. Nowadays, I don't have a clue what I'm going to do once I hit the stage."

His nightly performances, he says, have given new zest to the family bar. In the summer months, there are few places on earth to rival the energy of performing in Dingle.

But in winter, the town returns to some kind of normality. For David, only a city that never sleeps can match his ambition.

Last week, he phoned *The Kerryman* to tell of signing a contract that will bring his show, Velocity, to New York

– or Broadway, to be more precise. Excited and all as he was at realising his prime goal while still aged the right side of 25, there was a tinge of concern to his words.

He has always been one for setting and meeting targets. Inspired after his sister won a medal at a local feis, a six-year-old David wanted a medal of his own. As he was too young to play football, Irish dancing was his only means to achieving that first ambition. He tried it and, within four years, he was world champion.

What started almost 20 years ago with Therese O'Shea's dancing lessons has led to a November run in New York. Following that, it would seem there's little, if anything, left to achieve.

"I don't know how I'm going to follow this one," he says, his familiar smile stretching still further. "I know it sounds clichéd, but this is the only dream I've ever had.

"As a dancer, I never dreamed of River Dance, Lord of the Dance, or being part of someone's show; it was about dancing in my own show. And the only place I ever dreamed of bringing that show was Broadway. Who knows? Maybe I could do a longer run over there in future!"

Those not from this locality may remember David's ambitious performance in Britain's Got Talent last year and think only of Simon Cowell's lukewarm reaction – but David himself described it as one of his finest experiences.

It was an unfinished product, one he was never confident in, and the routine was heavily influenced by what the show's producers wanted. He speaks only positively, however, of Cowell and criticisms that would have unnerved most others.

"I didn't think I was ever going to win it, but the exposure made it, hands down, the best thing I've ever done," he says. "I was approached by producers, and I originally said no because I was in the middle of final-year exams.

"Eventually, after long-winded discussions over the phone, I said I'd give it a go. But I didn't have long to turn around between those phone calls and the first audition. It was an unfinished product.

"I always expected what Simon Cowell said because I was never fully convinced in that routine. But you have to take advantage of everything that's being offered to you. I went in with open ears, and you have to expect directors or producers to put their spin on your act. I let them, I listened, and I learned. It stood to me".

He's a long way from where he started, but even looking ahead to November 15 and the first day of his Broadway run, he still rhymes off the names of those who helped him years ago, and he does so with fluency not unlike those of his championship-winning steps. Lessons learned from Therese, Miriam O'Sullivan, Katherine O'Sullivan, Jimmy Smith, Triona Breen, and six years as Celtic Steps' lead dancer all helped build his success story, and he knows that.

Educated in an all-boys primary school, his love of dance could have left him at the mercy of teasing. His principal, Maura Flahive, helped him bypass that by offering pupils homework-free evenings upon his many wins; for Maura's help in bringing his schoolmates onside, he remains grateful to this day.

But it's not so much a time for reminiscence as it is for looking ahead. He'll collaborate with James Devine, and 'Velocity' draws on the support of some of the foremost talents in music as David charts the evolution of dance from its beginnings right up to something like the visual experience he served to millions through Britain's Got Talent. After taking promoters' eyes at last year's Edinburgh Fringe Festival, extensive negotiations led to a Broadway contract.

"Keeping the story quiet was painful," he says. "Even the cast didn't know. My cellist was out in Japan when he heard the news. I tried phoning him eight or nine times, couldn't get through to him, and when the news broke, he rang me and said, 'What the hell is this?'

"Another local, Seán Leahy, will travel over as well, and the team will do a few performances for schoolchildren in New York. Then it's on to November 15 and the first public show. I cannot wait."

The Kerryman, June 27, 2018.

Still competing, still winning, still enjoying.

I don't think I'm as active now, at 28, as athlete Jim O'Shea, who's 50 years my senior.

Before I visited him in Listry in 2019, my colleague, Sinead Kelleher, told me to be ready not to get out of there too quickly; Jim loves a chat. She was right.

She also said that he's one of her favourite interviewees. I have that in common with her as well.

MANY men in their 70s love sport; nothing unusual in that, nothing to set Listry's Jim O'Shea apart.

His interest is deeper than most, granted. There aren't many men his age who'd say they're "on a high" the morning after a Champions League game – at least not in Kerry, the home of Gaelic football.

Mind you, he's been a Tottenham Hotspur fan for nearly 60 years, and having seen few trophies in that time, he has earned his joy at seeing 'Spurs' qualify for a European semi-final last night.

But being a Tottenham fan isn't what sets him apart either, peculiar and all as it is.

What makes Jim different is that he still competes and still wins. He's still an athlete of national and international quality, days short of 77 years.

"I was born on May 15, 1942, so I'm coming up on 77. It's approaching too fast," he says.

"I come from a place called Batterfield, about four miles away…I went to a school still standing in a place called Longfield between Firies and Castlemaine, and me being lightly built, I wasn't made for football – so I looked at athletics. I proved reasonably good at running 100 yards, 200 yards at under-12, under-14, and I started out competing in the sports meetings I could cycle to.

"My club was the old athletic club in Farranfore, which went through good times and bad but was kept going by a shopkeeper and taxi driver by the name of John Crowley."

That's when the story started; when it'll end, no one yet knows. He was given the option in the 1980s of entering masters athletics for over 40s – nowadays for over 35s – and felt able to continue the journey. His success in the 37 years since passed justifies that call.

"If the Lord is good to me, I'll be a member of Farranfore/Maine Valley 60 years next year," he says. "I started competing in masters from around 1982 in the 100 metres, high jump, and long jump, and I've had some wonderful times.

"Last year, I won gold in the European indoor championships in Madrid; I was lucky enough to get the better of a man from Finland in the over-75s category.

"I was at the World Indoor Championships in Torun, a lovely city, one of the few in Poland where not one brick was touched during World War Two. I flew to Gdansk ahead of the games and took a 170-kilometres train journey for the princely sum of €7.

"I actually went four centimetres better in the long jump than I did in Madrid, but I finished fourth, outside the medals. But I did win bronze in the over-75s high jump with a jump of one metre and 25 centimetres."

As impressive as that is, as heartening as it is to see a 77-year-old rolling his shirt sleeves up and telling a reporter he wants to take at the garden on this sun-drenched afternoon, you could say his mind is even sharper than body.

Ahead of *The Kerryman*'s visit to his yellow dormer, Jim came across an old booklet with track-and-field results from the late 1800s to the 1940s. What was its relevance, his reason for showing it to this newspaper? *The Kerryman* printed it.

A copy of Athletics Weekly, a publication he buys weekly, is the next item he leafs through, and it holds similarly interesting content.

"Some results from the Masters Championship are towards the back, and my own name was there; I don't know was it last week or the week before last," he says.

"As you can see, there are some very good times and some very good throws, very good jumps. I see there's one set of results there from an over-90s category. There's no upper age limit for masters athletics.

"I have a great passion for athletics; I've been obsessed with following the results and statistics with many years. I have to buy Athletics Weekly every week, and I have to pick up the paper and read the sports pages every morning."

The late, great sportswriter Hugh McIlvanney liked to call sport "Our magnificent triviality", and it was an accurate description on most counts. Most of us like to follow the scores, scandals, offsides, and near-misses, but while sport enlivens lives, it rarely changes them. For Jim, sport has done both.

He hasn't an ache or a pain, and he feels staying active has helped in that regard. His passion for sport led to him meeting his wife – Anne, from Castlebar – at a dance hall following a major athletics meeting in Dublin in 1967, and they went on to have three sons, all of whom live locally.

In other words, sport was and is central to much of what's good in his life. He hasn't kept at light weights and gym exercises with Jerry Horgan in Killorglin without reward. He travels to Castleisland's An Ríocht weekly to better his jumping, but it also betters his life.

"I haven't an ache or a pain, and I think sport has played a big part, and I think it should be encouraged more with our young people. When I was in Torun, I don't think I saw one young obese person. I'm not being political, but I think successive sport ministries have failed in that we still don't have a proper PE programme embedded into the primary curriculum. We do seem to have a very poor attitude to healthy eating and exercise in this country.

"I've made friends through sport, too. I would regularly send off e-mails to British athletes I've competed against, even though I'm not very good with the computer. We're opponents on the day of the competition, but friendships do bloom afterwards – and that's the way it should be.

"I wonder – when I see sportspeople dropping out at 15, 16, retirements before 30 when they'd have previously gone on to 35 – if sport's still as fun as it should be. Because sport should be fun, first and foremost. Nowadays, it's a fierce commitment by people at the top... With masters, the enjoyment is still there, very much so.

"I'm lucky; it's easier for me to continue because Mrs O'Shea [Anne] is very supportive; we've even travelled to the British indoors together in London, and we meet our cousins on both sides when we're there.

"Even when I said I wanted to go to Madrid and Torun, she only said one thing: 'Why not?'."

The Kerryman, April 24, 2019.

A 'local' is nothing without the locals.

I met former Kerry footballer Billy O'Shea one Saturday morning, around the 10th anniversary of a fire that burned through his family's bar. His aunts – Rhetta and Ann – perished in the blaze.

It was a hammer blow, not just for Billy and his family and relatives; many of Killorglin's old stock, on Langford Street, were left without a community hub. Billy fought back, though.

IF you ever doubted the importance of community, a chat with Billy O'Shea wouldn't be long putting you right.

Everyone loves a comeback. He was probably involved in a fair few on the football field, be it with Kerry or Killorglin's Laune Rangers.

But sport is sport, and while many of us are inclined to treat it as more important than it is, what matters is elsewhere. Now and then, people experience things that force that point into sharp focus.

And when they happen, your friends and your family are key to pushing through.

What the O'Shea family sustained 10 years ago was the bitterest of blows. Flames ruined the bar and the building that's been in the family since the early 1900s, but graver still, of course, were the deaths of its residents, Billy's aunts: Rhetta McSwiney and Ann O'Shea.

"For the family, it was very hard because Rhetta and Ann didn't have any offspring," Billy says. "Their offspring, in effect, were their nieces and nephews, and for us, it was very, very hard to take. They were as good as mothers to us. We were very upset, very upset, when the whole thing happened.

"Some of the family are based outside the county, but every chance they got to come down here and help out, especially during Puck, they would, and they loved it. I felt sorry for them because they told me themselves they found it very hard to take. They don't really talk about it.

"It's a close-knit community here on Langford Street. It was as big a blow, if not bigger, to them than even the family as they would have known Rhetta and Ann throughout their whole lives.

"Everyone used to pop in, even to just say hello. It was that kind of set-up. I remember the night of the millennium, the whole street congregated here. It was more of a family gathering than a business – and that's the way it always was."

But within 14 months of the blaze, Billy had the bar open again. It was a quick turnover, he points out, considering the extent of what happened, and he's proud as well that "it was all locals involved in the building".

"Straight away," he says when asked when it was he decided to bring the premises back to life. "I didn't even consider not doing it, to be honest."

It's now 10 years since the fire and nine years since the bar's re-opening. The premises have a very different look today, but reminders of what came before are here. The words 'Rhetta's Retreat' sit over the entrance to the snug, and a plaque is also there in memory of Ann. The counter that's been there since the early 1900s, which remarkably survived the blaze, is its focal point.

Or at least it's the focal point in terms of furnishings. The real heart of the bar is the locality supporting it; its support was there throughout those 14 months and lives on today.

"It [the bar] looked very bad after the incident. You'd kind of be looking at it and saying, 'No, this isn't right at all'. Once everything had been settled, we got straight into it," Billy says. "They [the people of Langford Street] were very supportive when we decided to put it back up again, delighted really, because it was part of their livelihood. It was an institution.

"We didn't know what was going to happen when we put it back up; we just tried to continue as per the norm. Thankfully, it's still up and running after 10 years back. We've had fabulous support from the people. I think the family were all delighted to see it back up and running… It meant a lot to them to see that name continuing.

"We opened on July 23 the year after. Like any new venture, there was always going to be a honeymoon period, and there was one for a while. It lulled off for a bit, but it found its own niche after that. Since then, it's been tipping away nicely. As I say, it meant a lot to the people of the street because it was kind of a focal point for them."

Most of the work today is carried out by Billy and his wife, Emir, whom Billy says doesn't get the credit she deserves: "I'm only the front of the thing. She does all the work in the background that nobody sees."

She keeps the place clean, presentable, and by the looks of things today, she's doing a fine job.

But the main priority is continuing a legacy that stretches back to Billy's great-grandfather, and rewarding Langford Street's people for the loyalty they showed the O'Sheas in their time of need. They do this by giving them a 'local' that feels a little bit like home, just as it always did to Billy.

"Rhetta was the owner and reared me since I was 13, when I moved from Listowel to go to school here. I fell in love with Killorglin, and that was the reason I stayed here," he says.

"There's a lot of talk about the trade at the moment and the various laws in place. But I suppose you have to be inventive for the public and give them a reason to get together. That's what we're trying to do, always bring new ideas to the table.

"It's all community-oriented. It was always a part of the community and will, hopefully, remain that way. It's important for small towns to have a 'local', where they can meet people, have an outlet. I've always tried to create an atmosphere here where people can feel comfortable, be made to feel welcome, and a small bit at home."

The Kerryman, June 13, 2019.

Just Kerry doing Kerry things

Any Kerry news journalist will tell you that an election is to us what an All-Ireland final is to our sports reporters. They're such exciting, weird occasions.

In 2020, I covered my first General Election, and I did my best to capture that excitement and that weirdness.

AS the country voted in a way it's never done before – most notably by electing 37 Sinn Féin and 12 Green TDs – Kerry stuck to a more traditional formula: two Healy-Raes, one Sinn Féin, one Fine Gael, one Fianna Fáil.

Aside from a Green surge and a much-larger-than-usual share of the vote for Sinn Féin, it was another case of Kerry doing Kerry things.

But arriving at a familiar destination still called for a bumpy journey. The counting day – or days, in Kerry's case – is a blood sport, a faux circus, and as emotions are whipped up under the public's glare, weird things happen.

Danny Healy-Rae isn't known for scientific takes on environmental stuff, but he ramped that up to 12 by telling an actual planet – the one he lives on, no less – to go 'to Hell' on national television.

It was an unusually bullish statement coming from someone who hadn't guaranteed his election at that point, but one he promised he would "Make no apologies to anyone, anywhere for".

He apologised the next day.

To be fair to Healy-Rae – who cited a lack of sleep for his outburst – count centres are highly charged, and it takes, as Green candidate Cleo Murphy rightly put it, "a big person to row back on a comment". She's right: it can be hard for a mere person to say sorry, never mind a TD.

Count day has a reputation for entertainment – and as Healy-Rae proved, it does provide that – but when the thrill of tallying is done for and the wait for the inevitable sets in, a strange atmosphere takes hold.

In Kerry, that weird transition between the tallying and the first count lasted roughly seven hours.

So it was up to those in Killarney's Coral Leisure Centre to fill that void, and Sinn Féin supporters did more than most to break the monotony.

Buoyed by the knowledge that their candidate, Pa Daly, would clear the quota handily, Sinn Féin backers filled the hour-or-so leading up to the official announcement with unfurled flags and song: 'Come out ye Black and Tans', 'A Nation Once Again', and 'On the One Road' made up their repertoire. It won't have been an ice-breaker to appeal to all tastes, but it was a break from all the nothingness.

When the announcement of what we already knew did arrive – at around 10pm on Sunday, some seven hours after tallies concluded – Michael Healy-Rae and Daly were hoisted like Sam Maguire, as far above their supporters' shoulders as they were the quota.

Hooting, hollering, Puck Fair on a basketball court.

And then Pádraig Burke announced an adjournment. And then everyone left – very quickly. And then the sound of hailstones lashing the Coral Leisure Centre was all that was left to deny us silence.

Count results tumbled in at a faster pace on Monday, but it still took the best part of a day to fill three seats as transfers trickled from one candidate to the next.

We eventually met a result we'd all known was on its way for a day and a half. It was a long wait for the inevitable, but it at least gave us time to enjoy a few candidates' renditions of the 'Rose of Tralee', Monday's song of choice and a marked contrast to the Wolfe Tones' Sunday domination.

And then we left the bubble, the blood sport, the faux circus, and returned to planet earth; it was still there, as much as Danny had wished it away on Sunday.

The Kerryman, February 12, 2020.

Not so sisterly.

This might be the most bizarre story I've covered in the past five years. I learned one Wednesday evening that Dingle and Santa Barbara's Sister City relationship had broken down, and then I found myself trawling through local government records from California. It was all there, waiting to be written about – now I just needed to find out what Dingle thought of what had taken place eight time zones away.

Let's just say they weren't impressed.

THINGS tend to drag in January. Christmas has gone, it's not quite spring, and the world is recharging while it has the chance.

But there was plenty zip to a January 29 meeting of the Santa Barbara Sister Cities Board as a vote taken by one of its sub-committees earlier that month was written into the record.

This set in motion the severing of a special 17-year relationship between the Californian city and a small Kerry town; within three months, Santa Barbara's ties with Dingle would unravel, officially at least.

"The committee voted last night to recommend to Council and the Mayor to dissolve the Santa Barbara Dingle Sister City relationship," Pat Fallin stated. "We have requested numerous times in the past year to bring it [Dingle] in to compliance with the new guidelines adopted in 2019.

"Our delegation that visited in 2018 did not feel all that welcome. Many of the people they spoke with weren't even aware of Santa Barbara and Dingle being Sister Cities.

"The Sister City was founded in 2003, and there have been a couple of exchanges but very little reciprocity. The committee in Dingle is one couple and no other engagement with other members of the public or at the local government level."

Santa Barbara was now looking towards another "more viable" Irish Sister City.

On April 7, a city council resolution said "there have been minimal educational or cultural exchanges" between the two Sisters. "There have been no official visitors from the City of Dingle to the City of Santa Barbara" or vice versa in recent years, it added. The mayor received authority to dissolve the relationship.

It would be an embarrassment for any town or city, but for Dingle, a town that spins gold from tourism – much of it driven by US visitors – it's mortifying. Or it would be, at least, if the claims levelled against Dingle fared well under scrutiny.

"The committee had no inkling this [dissolution] was on the cards," Dingle-Santa Barbara Sister City Committee Secretary and Community Chair Máiréad de Staic tells *The Kerryman*. "They haven't contacted us in relation to that before, during, or after the process," she claimed.

She and her husband, Brian, are the "one couple" the Santa Barbara side referred to as being the entire Dingle committee. However, she says the board actually has six members – as well as some 30 representatives of different organisations – and that's far from being the sole point she wishes to challenge.

Having looked through material from both sides of the Atlantic, *The Kerryman* is aware of at least 12 delegations between the two sister cities, whether official or unofficial, since 2003. Almost half of these were educational or cultural delegations, and some received coverage on these pages or in Santa Barbara local media.

One Santa Barbaran source observed that 12 visits isn't a lot relative to other Sister City relationships – Santa Barbara also has sisters in Mexico, Greece, Japan, Philippines, and China – but to call the interaction between Dingle and its Californian sibling 'minimal' seems tough.

And to say there have been no recent visits between the two Sisters is untrue – unless one applies a very harsh definition of the word 'recent'.

Then-mayor Helene Schneider and seven others formed a delegation to Kerry in 2017; a group also visited in 2018; and in 2019, a Bank of Montecito group travelling the west of Ireland included Dingle on its tour.

A 13-strong business delegation represented Dingle on a visit to Santa Barbara in 2015, while Dingle International Film Festival showcased at the Santa Barbara equivalent in 2016 and made a presentation to the family of Gregory Peck, relatives of Lios Póil's Tomás Ághas. More recently, Máiréad, Brian, and their son, Dara, visited in 2018 after mudslides devastated Santa Barbara.

Ms de Staic claims the Dingle side knew nothing of moves to dissolve the relationship until contacted by Raidió na Gaeltachta last month. Following that, in an e-mail seen by *The Kerryman,* the Dingle side countered what Pat Fallin had stated.

They hit back at claims they were requested "numerous times in the past year" to adhere to new guidelines: "This has never been discussed or mentioned to anyone in Dingle save one email at the end of 2019 and a passing comment by Gil Garcia during their visitation…This [the e-mail] was answered by Máiréad de Staic the same day. However, her e-mail was neither responded to [nor] even acknowledged", they claimed.

They questioned how the 2018 delegation to Dingle "did not feel all that welcome": "This is an inexplicable statement…Upon their arrival in Dingle they were greeted by some 40 different organisations, clubs, businesses, schools, etc."

They attached what appears to be a Santa Barbara report, which wrote of this "amazing meeting with community members representing eclectic organizations, festivals, businesses, politics, authors, artists, craftsepeople & educators!"

Dingle responded to a statement that "They have resisted expanding [the Sister City relationship] to the larger County of Kerry": "This was only brought up to us just once – rather abruptly and without any context – in the middle of the large Dingle reception," they claimed.

"The gist of this proposal is to make the entire County of Kerry the sister city instead of Dingle, for reasons that were never explained clarified or even followed up upon".

On that point, Ms de Staic tells *The Kerryman* that "There isn't a city of Kerry. When they mentioned it to the people in Tralee, they got the same reply: it couldn't be done, it isn't a city, it's a number of big towns. And the Sister City relationship with Dingle was working perfectly well."

"The decision to challenge this decision originated in Santa Barbara," Ms de Staic says of what's to come next.

"We've been contacted by members and friends in Santa Barbara. On their instructions, letters were sent to the Mayor of Santa Barbara and City Council."

Letters were also sent recently to journalists and political figures on both sides of the Atlantic. Former Mayor Schneider, now a board member of Sister Cities International, is among those recipients.

On Thursday last, May 14, *The Kerryman* sent a set of queries to four separate e-mail addresses listed as Santa Barbara Sister Cities Board contacts. The following day, we sent the same queries to Pat Fallin. None of the five parties has responded yet.

There's irony in all this: President Eishenhower created the Sister Cities movement in 1956 as a means of bringing communities worldwide closer together.

Now it seems a town and city already eight timezones apart are drifting still further from one another.

The Kerryman, May 20, 2020.

Mike takes one last stop

If you saw Mike O'Neill once, you'd remember him forever. He ran the Railway Tavern Bar in Camp, but it's more likely you'll have known him for his long, wild beard.

The thing is, though, he was a lot more than a man with magnificent facial hair. He was a musician, he was an unofficial tour guide, he was stuck in everything – and he had some unique passions that set him still further apart.

His death followed a short illness. His Funeral took place during the COVID-19 pandemic, so a quiet send-off beckoned, but a few friends had other ideas.

THERE'S only one Mike O'Neill, and there'll only ever be one Mike O'Neill.

He was the bearded, spectacled proprietor of Camp's Railway Tavern Bar, and by dint of his warm personality and knowledge of his home patch, he was a tourism ambassador at the gateway to the Dingle Peninsula.

And he was so much more than that.

"He loved people, and people loved him," Camp's Brigid O'Connor said of Mike, the man who sat behind her all through school. "People will forget what you said, people will forget what you did, but people will never forget how you made them feel. And Mike Neill made everyone feel like a million dollars."

At 71 years, Mike O'Neill slipped away peacefully in University Hospital Kerry on Friday. By Monday – thanks to his children, his wife, and the hundreds who cared about him – a send-off as lovely as COVID-19 restrictions could allow was in place.

The miniature Volkswagens that decorate his bar were swapped for the real thing, and they led his cortège from his home to his grave in Camp's New Cemetery. His friends, hundreds of them, lined the route as he passed through. That'd be a sight in normal times, and these aren't normal times.

"When we realised he had passed away, I got on to Gene Finn, and between us, we pulled together all the many groups he was involved with," Brigid said. "Mountaineering, drama, the Camino walk, trad music – he was stuck in everything.

"They all wanted to take part, and the Gardaí gave us their blessing. We lined the route between his house and Camp post office, I'd say around 300 of us – and we still observed social distancing.

"We were not leaving Mike Neill go without a send-off. The COVID-19 wasn't going to beat us."

To understand why they did it, you'll need to understand Mike, whose tavern is part pub, part tribute to his unique set of passions.

You've the 'VW' miniatures: Volkswagen was his motor, and a second in 'The Railway' gets that point across.

"I got hooked on Monica [one of his first VWs, a '68 Beatle] and I'm with them since," he told a film crew a few years back. "I don't know is it the sound of them or the shape of them – I just like them".

He remembered the Old Dingle Railway, one of the few left who could, and though it shut when he was a youngster, his tavern doubled up as a kind of railway museum.

"If anyone came into the pub and was new or wasn't from the area, he made them off," Brigid said. "If people took interest in the memorabilia, he'd carry them off for the day and show them where it [the train] used to stop, where such and such an accident happened – he had it all off.

"He had a thing about trains. I think it started from going in and out of Jack O'Leary's house; he was the stationmaster, just across the way.

"He travelled the world, a lot of it by train – in fact, he crossed Canada just last year. I'm sure he'd have gone on a few more trips if fate hadn't intervened – because he still had plans, you know."

And it's true to say that Mike still had plans. He had walked most of the locality save for Maum to Annascaul, which was next on his checklist. Tralee Mountaineering Club will do it on his behalf instead.

He had also vowed that his bar wasn't staying shut beyond COVID. It would re-open in all its quirkiness.

But whatever about the ambitions he had for a future that wasn't meant to be, the locals have plans, too: to pay him an even bigger tribute than Monday's send-off.

"Everyone's shattered," Brigid said. "But one thing's for certain, there'll be a big celebration of his life when all this is over – and I tell you something, it'll be the biggest event ever seen on this peninsula.

"He wasn't a public persona, but he was as well-known as any president of the world here in Camp."

The Kerryman, May 27, 2020.

Lost in the Outback: what became of Paddy Moriarty?

Abbeyfeale man Paddy Moriarty (70) vanished from an Australian outback town of just 12 people in 2017. There isn't another sign of human life for dozens of miles around.

I first reported on this bizarre story in 2018, but it wasn't until late 2019 that I re-discovered it after Australian reporters Kylie Stevenson and Caroline Graham issued an appeal to this side of the world to find out more about Paddy's roots – which are also a bit of a mystery. I interviewed both reporters to find out more about this fascinating and grim story; I trawled through documents and reportage; and I also tried to help the duo find out more about Paddy's life pre-Australia.

This piece went on to win in the 'Feature Story of the Year' category of the 2019/20 Local Ireland Media Awards.

Last orders

On December 16, 2017, Paddy Moriarty left an Outback pub and leapt onto his quad bike. Glued to routine, he visited the Larrimah 'Pink Panther' Hotel daily to polish off eight tins of 'XXXX Gold,' a mid-strength lager, before taking the two-minute drive home.

His red kelpie, Kellie, sat to his back as they took the highway bisecting Larrimah, an Australian hamlet of a dozen people. It's two hours south of the next town and small enough to make Paddy's native Abbeyfeale look like London.

They made it home: Paddy's wallet, a cooked chicken he received from a tourist that Saturday evening, and his quad were all there when police arrived days later.

But there was no sign of 70-year-old Paddy. He and Kellie haven't been seen for two years.

Larrimah

"It's hard to imagine the emptiness of the landscape around Larrimah," Australian reporter Caroline Graham says.

"It was described to us as 'flat and featureless', which seem like mundane descriptors – but if you were to get lost there, those words are terrifying."

The Stuart Highway runs for 3,000 kilometres and divides Australia east and west; Larrimah's a rare speck of life along its monotonous, scrub-flanked Northern Territory stretch.

"The nearest fuel stop and grocery store are 90 kilometres away," says Caroline's colleague, Kylie Stevenson. "Because of this, Larrimah's pub wears many hats; it also acts as a caravan park, post office, restaurant, and bus stop."

The Pink Panther Hotel, Paddy's local, isn't luxurious but does its best to draw custom. It's bright pink to catch the eyes of highway motorists, and owner Barry Sharpe kept hundreds of exotic animals out back: primarily birds but also wallabies, snakes, lizards, and three crocodiles – one of whom has no eyes and is named after Ray Charles.

But while on a writing retreat in Larrimah three years ago, Kylie met a moustachioed Irishman who added as much Outback character as any of those creatures.

"I'd take a break from writing and wander into the pub, where I'd often find Paddy and his previous dog, Rover, having a few quiet beers," she says. "He was very friendly and always up for a yarn. I remember being surprised when he said he was originally from Ireland; he had no hint of an accent.

"He said he'd come to Australia [in 1966] on the Fairstar as a teenager and worked on cattle stations across the Top End. I remember asking him what his life in Ireland was like, and he said it was one of freezing cold and poverty.

"To me, he seemed like a typical Outback bloke: a guy who was comfortable living on the land, who was always up for a laugh with his mates, and happy to chat with anyone who wandered into the pub".

Looking for a body

Police say they first received a report three days after Paddy's disappearance, though Caroline believes one was possibly made sooner. Paddy didn't attend Sunday-morning 'Church' – he went to the pub to watch rural-affairs show 'Landline' weekly, a ritual that came to be known as Church – and Sharpe left to check on him. Paddy wasn't home, but nothing looked awry; it seemed as though he'd just popped out.

But residents' worries deepened as days slipped by.

Whenever that first report went in, police arrived in Larrimah on December 19 to a scene "completely undisturbed", with Paddy's vehicle and quad parked outside.

"The bed was made; he had food on the table; he had dog food for his dog, Kellie", Detective Sergeant Matt Allen told ABC television. "It's completely out of character for Paddy…He has a strict routine where he attends the pub, has eight beers a day, and comes home before dark".

Police searched on foot, on motorbike, and by helicopter, all the while battling offensive heat, harsh landscape, and even their emotions.

"Many of them knew Paddy and had spent time with him in the pub or working on stations together," Caroline says. "As the days wore on, the searchers must have been increasingly aware that they were running out of time; you simply couldn't be in that environment for long without realising how dangerously hot it is.

"They all spoke of the nightmarish realisation they were no longer looking for Paddy; they were looking for a body."

It's possible Paddy wandered off, got lost, or fell victim to Larrimah's terrain, which is said to include sinkholes. But Kellie had also vanished, and police combed the region but found nothing.

Sinister theories became the most plausible. Police called off the search on December 23, and a murder investigation began.

Local tensions

Larrimah's an accidental town. When funds ran dry for the North Australian Railway, intended to run the country's length, construction was called off a few miles south of Larrimah.

It, therefore, served as a railhead until the line closed in 1976, but community spirit kept things afloat after that. The town had a community veggie patch, a beautiful rail commemoration, and in 1998, its locals toasted a National Tidy Towns award.

Stranded in the Aussie Bush, residents had to fight for each other. Now they fight against each other.

As personalities clashed – for whatever reasons – cracks became breaks. Civic pride crumbled under claims of theft, arson, harassment, assault, vandalism, slander.

Residents argued over naming the town's two streets; over 'covert' speed-bump installation; over ownership of a buffalo that was shot and eaten. By 2004, the town's once-exemplary progress association had split into two groups.

And the venom dripped into matters beyond town upkeep. Some people liked Paddy; others didn't.

Fran Hodgetts ran a tea house across from Paddy's house, and she used everything from crocodile to buffalo to camel as pie filling. She faced allegations of using Paddy as an ingredient, but forensic examinations uncovered "no evidence...whatsoever" to support such a revolting theory.

But there was tension between Ms Hodgetts and Paddy; he warned tourists off her pies and told national television his dog would avoid her food.

"Look, Paddy had thrown a kangaroo under her window, probably more than once," Sharpe told Kylie and Caroline's podcast series, 'Lost in Larrimah', in 2018.

"One time, a donkey got run over...Paddy went and cut its penis off and threw that up her driveway."

"In Katherine Local Court in October 2016, Fran claimed that Paddy poisoned her palm trees, stole her umbrella, abused her customers, destroyed her furniture, and cut the cord to her security cameras," Kylie says.

"One night, she says, he put a newspaper cut-out of her under her fence, smeared in human faeces."

Paddy denied the allegations and the judge dismissed the case. Ms Hodgetts had no proof.

She shared insults with more locals than Paddy, though; her fury at others selling pastries is well-known, and police also said the majority of past call-outs to Larrimah stemmed from arguments she had with her ex-husband, not with Paddy. She didn't like the Abbeyfeale man but stoutly and consistently denies any part in his disappearance.

"I don't know where he is", she told ABC television in 2018, "and I'm not sad that he's gone".

Life before emigrating:

No one knows what happened to Paddy after December 2017, and details of his life pre-Australia are similarly vague. He left Ireland in the mid-'60s, aged just 19 – and we don't know much else. Even his birth cert – obtained by police – takes some decoding thanks to the registrar's cramped, knotted handwriting.

Paddy was born in Limerick County Hospital, Croom, on March 30, 1947, and while there's no record of a father, his mother was Mary Teresa Moriarty of Dromtrasna O'Brien, Abbeyfeale.

"She died in 1995," Caroline says. "A number of people in Ireland – and Irish-born people living elsewhere – have recognised her name and come forward as potential relatives…However, none of them have specific memories of Paddy, so it's possible he might have been adopted, fostered, or spent time in a care facility.

"Police have even done some DNA testing but haven't found conclusive evidence of a familial link – which is not uncommon in these circumstances.

"Paddy doesn't have a next of kin in Australia and, although he told some people that he had children with an Afghan-Aboriginal woman he met while working on a cattle station, he is not listed on the birth certificate of any child.

"So for his friends in Australia and police, finding a relative or link to his life in Ireland has become very important. Particularly in a case like this, where there's so little closure".

Limerick Councillor Francis Foley is Paddy's cousin: his grandmother and Paddy's grandfather were siblings.

Foley may have met Paddy's mother, but he can't be sure. If he did, he was too young then to remember it now.

"I met one or two of Mary's sisters, and I knew of her," he says. "I might've met her, but when you're 12, 14, 15, it means nothing and doesn't stick in your head.

"She moved away at some stage, and I didn't even know of Paddy until I heard he'd gone missing. But, yes, from what we know, he was from Abbeyfeale.

"I think there's a cousin of Mary's living in Limerick city as well. I have another first cousin here in town, and some of the Moriartys are living in England. I understand it was one of them who provided DNA. I haven't given DNA, but if Australian police ask, I'd have no problem whatsoever."

When news arrived that 'one of their own' was missing, Abbeyfeale took note. Some commented on Paddy's likeness to Pattie – his grandfather – and other members of the Moriarty family. But no one remembers Paddy, and there's no evidence to confirm he returned after 1966.

"It caused fascination, especially when the story broke two years ago," Foley says. "To think what might've happened him, it's very sad. There's no sign or trace of him.

"At this stage, there might never be."

Loose ends

The local dump became part of Paddy's routine after he moved into town in 2006. Every morning, he'd walk there with his dog before helping Sharpe with jobs at the pub, for which he received a carton of beer at the weekend.

Police combed this dump for evidence but found none. Divers, detectives, and forensic investigators also searched the local dam, but to no avail. Police even probed the whispers that one of the Pink Panther's crocodiles had eaten Paddy but found nothing to support that theory.

"The wild donkeys outnumber residents," Kylie says of Larrimah's wildness. "You'll also find giant feral pigs, buffalo, many birds of prey, and lots of venomous snakes.

"Given the couple of days it took to report Paddy's disappearance, it's possible if he had wandered off, encountered a snake, or had a medical emergency of some kind that wild animals could have interfered with remains.

"But police are confident they still would've found something – his clothing or his dog, Kellie – had this happened."

Police have questioned everyone in Larrimah since December 2017, and everyone denies involvement.

In mid-2018, an inquest began two hours north in Katherine. It was unusually soon to hold a sitting, but because most people in Larrimah are aged the wrong side of 70, it was necessary.

"The main event at the inquest was the appearance of Owen Laurie," Kylie says. "By the time of the inquest, he'd lived in the town for around eight months; none of the residents there could even say what he looked like."

Laurie was Ms Hodgetts' gardener at the time Paddy vanished. ABC reported he and Paddy argued over their dogs days beforehand, though Mr Laurie denied any aggression.

"Owen said 'There's going to be trouble,'" Ms Hodgetts told the inquest. "I said, 'don't do anything stupid…I don't want to come back and see you in jail'."

According to Russell Marks' report for The Monthly, Laurie listed his ailments "to illustrate why he couldn't have jumped a fence and attacked Moriarty". He also attempted calls from Larrimah's telephone box that evening, but police believe those calls were unrelated to the disappearance.

"I swear to God, that man [Laurie] is as honest as the day is long," Ms Hodgetts said. "I love him to pieces as a person." Mr Laurie denies involvement in Paddy's disappearance. The inquest was adjourned and is yet to resume. It's been held open to allow further evidence.

Larrimah today

Larrimah was teetering as things were. Then Paddy disappeared, and further pain followed. Barry Sharpe sold the Pink Panther in 2018 and said at the time that he had terminal cancer. He died last month. Fran Hodgetts also received a cancer diagnosis and has left town for treatment. She's unlikely to return, local reportage states.

Police can't say much about their persons-of-interest list except to say they have persons of interest – some of whom are from outside Larrimah – and the list remains unchanged from last year. The same can't be said for Larrimah.

"Paddy is a palpable absence in Larrimah," Caroline says. "His house is under the care of the public trustee, and there is a huge sign with his picture on it out front, pleading with travellers for information."

Police have no official suspects. They've vowed to continue their investigations for as long as it takes – but two years on, there's no sign anyone's much closer to solving the Paddy Moriarty mystery.

The Kerryman, January 1, 2020.

The boy who played his way to heaven

My uncle and namesake, Tadhgie Evans, died in a tragic accident in Lios Póil when he was just eight and a half years old. On his 50th anniversary in April 2021, I wrote a tribute to him based on what I'd been told about him. With permission from my grandfather, dad, aunt, and uncles, it was published the following Wednesday in The Kerryman.

I WRITE this on April 3, a Saturday, the exact date and day on which a little boy died 50 years ago in Lios Póil. It happened in the townland I live in.

Of course, I never met this boy, but he's had a more profound impact on my life than most people I have met. I hear about him all the time. I'm even named after him.

That's because he was my uncle: Tadhgie.

He was only eight years and eight months on that day in 1971, and he was playing at the time, as he usually was. Tadhgie died in a tragic accident on a rope swing.

We could reflect on the 50 years that he hasn't been here, but that doesn't seem right when we can talk about the nearly nine years he did live – because he certainly did *live*.

I didn't meet him, but his immediate family – my grandparents, my uncles, my aunt, my dad – had that fortune, and thanks to them, I can tell you about Tadhgie, or a little bit about him at least. So the words on this page aren't really mine; I'm just re-telling what I've been told by those who loved him.

My granda is Tommy and my nana was Kathleen, and Tadhgie – born on July 21, 1962 – was the middle child of their five. He is survived today by his dad (now over 90 years) and four siblings: Liam, Pádraig – that's my dad – Tomás, and Áine.

They were very different times in our village – it's not a village; that's just what we call our townland – and there were a lot more children running around the place, playing. And by the sounds of it, nobody played more than Tadhgie. My dad often told me that, looking back, it was almost as if Tadhgie sensed he wouldn't be around for long. He had no time for homework, not when there was so much fun, roguery, and good-natured devilment to be had in a village that sounds much louder than the one I live in today.

There was no football or soccer here, or not much of it at least. 'Hide and Go Seek' and 'Cowboys and Indians' were the games of choice instead, I gather. While any photo I've seen of Tadhgie had his bright, blonde hair on show, I'm told a cowboy hat often covered it up. He had a holster for his toy gun, and I suppose all of those details point to where his loyalties stood when it came to playing 'Cowboys and Indians'.

No piece of scrap timber and nothing resembling a wheel was safe from the young villagers, either. Who owned these materials was of no concern to them; if they were needed for assembling a buggy, onto a buggy they went.

Thanks to all of these games, the village children knew every blade of grass around them. But I'm told Tadhgie was the earliest riser in the Evans house each morning as every minute of daylight was a minute to play, and any minute not spent playing was a minute wasted.

He was like that for eight and a half years, right up to the end. On April 1, two days before he died, he called over to a neighbour, Paddy, and beckoned him to help his father; one of my granda's cows was having trouble calving. Paddy was milking his herd at the time, but he was a good neighbour, so that didn't matter. He upped and left.

But there was no cow when Paddy arrived back, just Tadhgie: "Got you, Paddy. You know today's the first of April?"

Paddy didn't like being made an 'April Fool' of, but he ought to have known better. This was Tadhgie he was dealing with.

On the day he died, April 3, he was looking forward to going to a neighbour's house to watch that evening's Eurovision Song Contest, which was being held in Dublin for the first time – but if he didn't know his maths tables, that wouldn't be happening.

As it happens, this was one of those rare days on which Tadhgie had all the answers when questioned by his mom, my nana. He had done his school work, it seemed.

She found out otherwise, a few weeks later, when she was looking through his school books. He had written the answers on the back of the tables' book she was reading from. Of course he had.

That was Tadhgie, I'm told, and many of these stories came to me from nana herself.

She told me that his life was short but fun-filled. "He played his way to Heaven," she often said to me.

Everyone else who remembers him – be they family; neighbours; or former teachers and schoolmates of his at the now-closed Clooncurra National School – tells me the same.

And maybe that's what we should think of when we think of him.

Nana left us to be with him in 2009, and I'm sure she'll never let go of him again.

I do wish I could have seen her reading this, though. I think she'd have liked it.

The Kerryman, April 7, 2021.

About the Author

Tadhg Evans hails from Lios Póil in County Kerry and attended school locally at Scoil Naomh Eoin Baiste and later Pobalscoil Chorca Dhuibhne in Dingle.

Thereafter, he went on to study Journalism at NUI Galway in 2016 and began his reporting career at The Kerryman in May of that year.

He has since gone on to become an award-winning journalist having picked up a Local Ireland Media Award in the Feature Story of the Year category. He won that prize in 2020 on the back of an in-depth investigation into the disappearance of Abbeyfeale native Paddy Moriarty from a tiny Australian Outback village three years ago.

In 'A Storied Kingdom', Tadhg's first book, he combines many of his passions, not least anything sport-related or Kerry-related.

As a board member of CLG Lios Póil himself, his knowledge of the GAA world shines through whenever he commits pen to paper on the subject. Hailing as he does from the Corca Dhuibhne Gaeltacht, he is a fluent Irish speaker and an advocate of a language that seems to face threats from all angles. More than anything else, though, he loves meeting people who have a story to tell – and that's exactly what drew him towards a life in journalism to begin with.

Printed in Great Britain
by Amazon